FOODS AND FLAVORS OF SAN ANTONIO

Foods and Flavors of San Antonio

Gloria Chadwick

PELICAN PUBLISHING COMPANY
Gretna 2009

The word "Pelican" and the depiction of a pelican are trademarks of Pelican Publishing Company, Inc., and are registered in the U.S. Patent and Trademark Office.

Library of Congress Cataloging-in-Publication Data

Chadwick, Gloria.
Foods and flavors of San Antonio / Gloria Chadwick.
p. cm.
Includes index.
ISBN 978-1-58980-646-7 (pbk. : alk. paper) 1. Mexican American cookery. 2. Cookery—Texas—San Antonio. I. Title.
TX715.2.S69C47 2009
641.59764'351—dc22
2008051393

Printed in the United States of America

Published by Pelican Publishing Company, Inc.
1000 Burmaster Street, Gretna, Louisiana 70053

For Jennifer, Jaime, Antonio, Jordan, Hannah, and Lindsey

Contents

Tex-Mex Tour ... 9
Appetizers ... 15
Beverages ... 29
Breakfast ... 37
Salads ... 53
Soups and Stews ... 59
Veggies, Beans, and Rice ... 71
Sandwiches, Quesadillas, and Tacos ... 97
Chili ... 121
Enchiladas ... 133
Beef and Pork ... 149
Chicken ... 173
Seafood ... 197
Breads and Tortillas ... 207
Seasonings, Salsas, and Sauces ... 213
Sweets and Treats ... 225
Index ... 238

Tex-Mex Tour

I moved to San Antonio in 2004 and began exploring all the sights, foods, fiestas, and flavors that make San Antonio the Tex-Mex capital of the world. There are so many things to do and see here, and this brief Tex-Mex tour will highlight the foods and flavors that make our city special.

Remember the Alamo? How could one forget? The Alamo represents the battle for freedom that was fought on March 6, 1836. The Alamo is perhaps the most famous spot in Texas. At this site, 189 defenders were overcome after repeated attacks by Mexican general Antonio López de Santa Anna's army. Originally named Misión San Antonio de Valero, the Alamo was established in 1718 as the city's first mission. Web site: www.thealamo.org.

Next on the Tex-Mex tour is the Tower of the Americas, built for HemisFair '68, San Antonio's World's Fair. Go up nearly six hundred feet to the top to enjoy the 360-degree view of the city and surrounding area. Among the grounds of HemisFair Park are beautiful water gardens and lushly landscaped areas. Web site: www.toweroftheamericas.com.

Visit Market Square, also known as El Mercado, where you'll find everything from tourist T-shirts to authentic Mexican imports. Browse through the thirty-two indoor specialty shops, enjoy the stage show with Mexican dancers and mariachi bands, then walk across the street and visit the eighty outdoor sidewalk vendors and cafés on Produce Row and Farmers Market Plaza. Web site: www.marketsquaresa.com.

Another famous sight and a great place to explore the foods and flavors of San Antonio is the River Walk or Paseo del Rio. You can stroll along the River Walk or take a boat cruise on the San Antonio River (www.riosanantonio.com). Enjoy the sizzling fajitas and frozen margaritas at one of the outdoor cafés. Web site: www.thesanantonioriverwalk.com.

Brackenridge Park offers 343 acres of outdoor activities, including a golf course and a miniature train ride. Within the grounds of the park are the Japanese Tea Gardens—a lush, year-round garden and floral display featuring shaded walkways, stone bridges, a six-foot waterfall, and ponds. Also located in the park is the San Antonio Zoo (www.sa-zoo.org), which is ranked one of the best zoos in the nation with over thirty-five hundred animals. Web site: www.wildtexas.com/parks/bracken.php.

Next on the tour is the San Antonio Botanical Garden. This thirty-three-acre lavish, beautiful garden offers a serene native forest walk, exotic plants from around the world, aquatic garden pools, glass pyramids, and an authentic log cabin. Web site: www.sabot.org.

If you're in the mood for a museum that both you and the kids will enjoy, visit the cultural and kid-friendly Witte Museum, which focuses on South Texas history and features historic artifacts, Texas art, and a wildlife diorama. Web site: www.wittemuseum.org.

Walk through La Villita, which means little village, to see local artists display and sell their colorful artwork. La Villita was San Antonio's first neighborhood and is now a beautiful historic arts village where you can shop, dine, or just take a peaceful walk. Web site: www.lavillita.com.

Probably the best and most scenic way to get around historical San Antonio is by taking a trolley tour of the city. Traveling through the sights is a breeze on the VIA trolley, an open air, authentic reproduction of a rail streetcar that traveled the streets of San Antonio more than fifty years ago. Four streetcar routes stop at downtown locations such as the Alamo, HemisFair Park, Market Square, Brackenridge Park, the Japanese Tea Gardens, the San Antonio Zoo, the San Antonio Botanical Garden, and other historical sites as well as shopping at Rivercenter Mall. Web site: www.viainfo.net.

Speaking of shopping, you might enjoy visiting North Star Mall, featuring the giant cowboy boots (www.northstarmall.com); Rivercenter Mall next to the River Walk (www.shoprivercenter.com); LaCantera (www.theshopsatlacantera.com); the outdoor Alamo

Quarry Market with the huge smokestacks (www.quarrymarket.com); or the beautiful Los Patios, featuring many specialty shops, which offer Mexican jewelry and south-of-the-border items (www.lospatios.com).

Want more culture? Next is Mission Trail, which includes four missions and the Alamo. The Mission San José was established in 1720 and is still an active mission, featuring a Mariachi Mass every Sunday. These missions, including the Mission Concepción, especially noted for its wall paintings; Mission San Juan, with its magnificent bell tower and elaborate alter; and Mission Espada, with its displays of how local Indians were educated in blacksmithing, woodworking, and other vocational areas, are all accessible via the six-mile Hike and Bike Trail. Web site: www.nps.gov/saan.

And, then there are our festivals. Let me tell you about Fiesta: Fiesta means party, and we San Antonians know how to party. Fiesta is the biggest and the best. This ten-day event features more than 150 events and activities, starting with the Fiesta Oyster Bake; continues with a carnival; plenty of Tex-Mex food; the Texas Cavalier's River Parade; the nighttime Fiesta Flambeau Parade; and ends with the Battle of Flowers Parade. Night in Old San Antonio (NIOSA), held in La Villita, draws thousands of people to party in the streets. Web site: www.fiesta-sa.com.

The Texas Folklife Festival, held annually in June on the fairgrounds of the Institute of Texan Cultures, reflects the cultures, foods, and lifestyles that make up San Antonio. Web site: www.texasfolklifefestival.org.

Since San Antonio is the birthplace of chili, the annual Return of the Chili Queens, held at Market Square in May features—you guessed it!—chili, with a variety of chili dishes for tasting and also a chili cook-off.

The River Walk hosts the annual Mud Festival in January, when the San Antonio River is drained and cleaned, as well as a Mardi Gras Festival in February; the St. Patrick's Day River Parade in March, when the river is dyed green; and the Children's Fiesta in April.

If you want to see a rodeo, go to the San Antonio Stock Show and Rodeo in February and see Texas cowboys. There are many events, including calf roping and bull riding. Attend the cowboy breakfast to kick off the rodeo, with free breakfast tacos and biscuits with gravy served at the Pro Bass Shops. Web site: www.sarodeo.com.

To get an authentic taste and feel for the foods and flavors of San Antonio, visit the Houston Street Fair and Market, held the last Saturday of every month. The fair features carnival rides, face painting, storytelling, hand-made art and crafts by local artists, drinks, food, and more. Web site: www.houstonstreetfairandmarket.com.

For more information about the attractions and festivals in San Antonio, please visit the San Antonio Convention & Visitors Bureau Web site at www.visitsanantonio.com. To learn more about the foods and flavors of the city, visit http://foodsandflavorsofsanantonio.blogspot.com.

Then there are the recipes that offer the true Tex-Mex flavor of San Antonio . . .

Foods and Flavors of San Antonio

Abbreviations

STANDARD			METRIC		
tsp.	=	teaspoon	ml.	=	milliliter
tbsp.	=	tablespoon	l.	=	liter
oz.	=	ounce	g.	=	gram
qt.	=	quart	kg.	=	kilogram
lb.	=	pound	mg.	=	milligram

Standard-Metric Approximations

⅛ teaspoon			=	0.6 milliliter
¼ teaspoon			=	1.2 milliliters
½ teaspoon			=	2.5 milliliters
1 teaspoon			=	5 milliliters
1 tablespoon			=	15 milliliters
4 tablespoons	=	¼ cup	=	60 milliliters
8 tablespoons	=	½ cup	=	118 milliliters
16 tablespoons	=	1 cup	=	236 milliliters
2 cups			=	473 milliliters
2½ cups			=	563 milliliters
4 cups			=	946 milliliters
1 quart	=	4 cups	=	.94 liter

Solid Measurements

½ ounce			=	15 grams
1 ounce			=	25 grams
4 ounces			=	110 grams
16 ounces	=	1 pound	=	454 grams

Appetizers

Beef Chimichangas

Chimichangas are little tortilla packets filled with beef, chicken, or cheese that are fried or baked until crisp.

1 lb. lean ground beef
1 tsp. cumin
1 tsp. oregano
3 tbsp. chili powder
1 tsp. black pepper
1 garlic clove, crushed
¼ cup chopped green chiles
¼ cup sour cream
½ cup butter
8 8" flour tortillas
1 cup grated cheddar cheese

Preheat the oven to 500 degrees.

Place the ground beef, cumin, oregano, chili powder, black pepper, garlic, and green chiles in a 12" skillet. Cook over medium heat until the beef is browned. Drain.

Remove the pan from the heat and stir in the sour cream.

Melt the butter in a separate 10" skillet over medium heat. Using tongs, dip both sides of each tortilla into the butter. Drain off the excess.

Place ⅓ cup of the filling on the center of each tortilla. Fold the tortillas into square packets. Place seam side down in a 13x9" baking dish. Bake for 15 minutes or until crisp.

Remove the chimichangas from the oven and sprinkle with cheese. Return to the oven and bake for 2 more minutes to melt the cheese.

Serves 8

Chicken Chimichangas

2 skinless, boneless chicken breasts
1 chipotle chile, seeded
1 tbsp. vegetable oil
2 small onions, finely chopped
4 garlic cloves, crushed
½ tsp. ground cumin
½ tsp. ground coriander
½ tsp. ground cinnamon
½ tsp. ground cloves
1 16 oz. can tomatillos, drained and chopped
2 15.5 oz. cans pinto beans, drained and rinsed
Salt and black pepper to taste
8 10" flour tortillas
¼ to ½ cup oil, for frying

Place the chicken breasts in a large saucepan, cover with water and add the chipotle chile. Bring to a boil, then reduce the heat and simmer for 10 minutes or until the chicken is cooked through and the chile has softened.

Remove the chile and chop it finely. Set aside.

Remove the chicken breasts and put them on a plate. Let cool slightly, then shred with two forks. Set aside.

Heat 1 tbsp. vegetable oil in a 12" skillet over medium heat. Add the onions and sauté until soft, about 3 minutes, then add the garlic, cumin, coriander, cinnamon, and cloves. Cook for 3 more minutes, stirring.

Add the tomatillos and pinto beans. Cook for 5 more minutes, stirring constantly to break up the tomatillos and some of the beans.

Add the chopped chipotle chile. Reduce the heat to low and simmer for 5 more minutes.

Add the shredded chicken. Season with salt and pepper to taste.

Stack the tortillas together and cover with plastic wrap. Place in the microwave and cook for 30 seconds.

Spoon the filling into the center of each warmed tortilla. Fold in both sides, then fold the bottom of the tortilla up and the top down to form a square packet. Moisten with water around the edges to seal.

Heat the ¼ cup oil in a 2" deep skillet and fry the chimichangas in batches until crisp, turning once. Remove with a slotted spoon and drain on paper towels.

Serves 8

Beef 'n' Black Bean Platter

1½ lb. lean ground beef
1 large onion, chopped
2 garlic cloves, chopped
¼ cup chili powder
2 tsp. oregano
2 15 oz. cans black beans, drained and rinsed
1 16 oz. package frozen corn, thawed
2 8 oz. cans tomato sauce
Juice of 1 lime
Salt and black pepper to taste
Tortilla chips
1 cup shredded cheddar cheese

Heat a 12" skillet over medium-high heat. Add the meat, onion, and garlic. Season the meat with the chili powder and oregano while it is cooking.

Add the beans, corn, and tomato sauce. Stir well to mix. Bring to a boil, then reduce the heat. Cover and simmer for 10 minutes.

Add the lime juice. Stir to mix. Season with salt and pepper to taste.

Line a serving platter with the tortilla chips. Spoon the beef mixture over and top with cheese.

Serves 12

Black Bean Caviar

This is San Antonio's version of caviar.

2 15 oz. cans black beans, drained and rinsed
1 10 oz. can diced tomatoes and green chiles, drained
1 garlic clove, minced
1 small onion, finely chopped
2 tbsp. olive oil
2 tbsp. lime juice
¼ tsp. salt
¼ tsp. ground cumin
1 8 oz. package cream cheese, softened
3 green onions, chopped
1 medium tomato, chopped
2 tbsp. chopped fresh cilantro
Tortilla chips or crackers

In a medium-size bowl, combine the black beans, tomatoes with green chiles, garlic, onion, olive oil, lime juice, salt, and cumin. Cover and refrigerate for 2 hours.

Spread the softened cream cheese onto a serving platter. Spoon the bean mixture evenly over the cream cheese.

Sprinkle the chopped green onions, tomato, and cilantro over the top.

Serve with tortilla chips or crackers.

Serves 12

Black Bean Dip

This black bean dip also makes a wonderful side dish accompaniment for a dinner.

2 15 oz. cans black beans, drained and rinsed
8 roma tomatoes, seeded and chopped
2 tbsp. red wine vinegar
3 tbsp. olive oil
1 cup chopped green onions
1 tbsp. fresh cilantro, chopped
¼ tsp. ground cumin
2 garlic cloves, minced
1 jalapeño pepper, seeded and finely chopped
Salt and black pepper to taste
Tortilla chips

Mix all the ingredients except the tortilla chips together in a medium-size bowl. Chill for 3 to 4 hours.

Serve with tortilla chips.

Serves 12

Cheesy Chorizo Bean Dip

Chorizo is a spicy sausage used in many Tex-Mex dishes.

½ lb. chorizo sausage
1 8 oz. package cream cheese
1¼ cups shredded cheddar cheese, divided
½ 15 oz. can black beans, drained, rinsed, and slightly mashed, or ½ 16 oz. can refried beans
1 10 oz. can diced tomatoes with chiles, drained (mild or hot according to your preference)
Fresh cilantro sprigs
Tortilla chips

Cook the chorizo sausage in a 10" skillet over medium heat. Drain and set aside.

Preheat the oven to 350 degrees. Spray a 9" baking dish with nonstick cooking spray. Set aside.

In a medium-size saucepan, warm the cream cheese over low heat until softened.

Add 1 cup of the cheddar cheese, the cooked chorizo, black beans, and tomatoes with chiles. Mix well.

Place this mixture in the prepared baking dish. Bake for 20 minutes or until bubbly.

Place the dip in an attractive bowl for serving. Top with the remaining cheddar cheese and a few sprigs of cilantro. Serve the tortilla chips on the side.

Serves 8

Note: If you're wondering what to do with the remaining beans, see the recipes for **Grilled Chicken Strip Salad**, page 53, or **Black Bean Burgers**, page 98.

Chorizo Bean Dip

This easy-to-prepare dip is loaded with flavor. It also tastes wonderful topped with Monterey jack cheese and wrapped in a soft, warm flour tortilla for a light lunch or snack.

½ lb. chorizo sausage
2 15 oz. cans black beans, drained, rinsed, and slightly mashed
Tortilla chips

Cook the chorizo in a 12" skillet over medium-high heat. Drain. Reduce the heat to low.

Add the black beans and heat through.

Serve with tortilla chips.

Serves 8

Chorizo Cheese Dip

½ lb. chorizo sausage
¼ cup finely chopped onion
1 cup salsa
3 cups shredded Monterey jack cheese, divided
1 avocado, diced
1 large tomato, diced
Tortilla chips

Preheat the oven to 350 degrees.

Cook the chorizo in a 12" skillet over medium heat. Halfway through cooking, add the onion. Drain.

Add the salsa, reduce the heat to low, and simmer for 10 minutes.

Spread 1½ cups of the cheese over the bottom of a 9x6" baking dish. Cover with the chorizo mixture. Sprinkle the remaining cheese on top. Bake for 10 minutes or until bubbly.

Top with the diced avocado and tomato. Serve with the tortilla chips.

Serves 8

Queso Chili Dip

This dip is easy and flavorful.

1 16 oz. box Velveeta cheese, cubed
1 10 oz. can diced tomatoes with chiles
Tortilla chips

Melt the cheese in a medium saucepan over medium heat. Add the tomatoes and heat through. Serve with tortilla chips.

Serves 12

Seven-Layer Dip

This dip is very popular in San Antonio. It's sold in all the grocery stores. Many Tex-Mex cookbooks make mention of it.

1 16 oz. can refried beans
1 cup guacamole
1 8 oz. container sour cream
3 roma tomatoes, diced
½ red onion, diced
1½ cups shredded cheddar cheese
½ cup chopped black olives
Tortilla chips

Evenly spread the refried beans over the bottom of a 9x9" glass baking dish. Cover and refrigerate for 15 minutes.

Spread the guacamole evenly over the beans.

Spread the sour cream over the guacamole.

Sprinkle the diced tomatoes over the sour cream.

Sprinkle the onion over the tomatoes.

Sprinkle the cheese on top of the onion.

Sprinkle the olives over the cheese.

Refrigerate for 1 hour before serving. Serve with tortilla chips.

Serves 8

Tex-Mex Bean Dip

1 16 oz. can refried beans
1 1.25 oz. package taco seasoning mix
¼ tsp. Tabasco® sauce
1 8 oz. container sour cream
1 4.5 oz. can chopped green chiles, drained
½ cup diced avocado
1 cup shredded cheddar cheese
½ cup diced green onion
½ cup chopped tomato
Nachos, Doritos®, or Tortilla chips

In a medium-size bowl, combine the beans with the taco seasoning mix and the Tabasco® sauce. Stir until blended.

Spread the bean mixture on a serving platter.

Spread the sour cream over the bean mixture to cover.

Layer the chiles, avocado, cheese, green onion, and tomato over the sour cream.

Cover and refrigerate for at least 4 hours. Serve with your choice of chips.

Serves 8

Chicken Empanadas

1 15 oz. box refrigerated pie crusts, containing 2 11" rounds
1 cup water
1 chicken bouillon cube
1 skinless, boneless chicken breast, coarsely chopped
1 4 oz. package cream cheese
2 tbsp. freshly chopped cilantro
4 tbsp. salsa
½ tsp. ground cumin
½ tsp. salt
¼ tsp. garlic powder
1 medium egg, beaten
Additional salsa for serving

Remove the pie crust pouches from the box. Let stand at room temperature for 15 to 20 minutes.

Heat the water and bouillon cube in a saucepan to boiling. Add the chicken. Reduce the heat to simmer and cook for 10 minutes to poach. Remove the chicken to a plate and finely chop. Set aside.

Heat the cream cheese in a small saucepan over low heat. Stir until melted.

Add the cilantro, salsa, cumin, salt, and garlic powder. Stir until smooth.

Stir in the chicken and remove the pan from the heat.

Unfold the pie crusts and remove the plastic film. Roll out slightly on a lightly floured surface. Cut into 3" rounds using a biscuit cutter. Reroll the pie crust scraps to make additional rounds.

Preheat the oven to 425 degrees. Line a baking sheet with aluminum foil.

Place about 2 tsp. of the chicken mixture in the center of each round. Brush the edges lightly with water. Pull one side of the dough over the filling to form a half circle. Pinch the edges to seal or press them together with the tines of a fork.

Place the empanadas on the prepared baking sheet. Brush lightly with the beaten egg. Bake for 16 to 18 minutes or until lightly browned. Serve with salsa.

Serves 12

Chorizo Crescents

1 lb. chorizo sausage
1 small onion, chopped
1 8 oz. package cream cheese
2 roma tomatoes, chopped
2 8 oz. cans crescent rolls

Preheat the oven to 350 degrees.

Cook the chorizo and onion in a 12" skillet over medium heat. Drain.

Take the pan off the heat. Add the cream cheese. Stir until the cheese is melted and the mixture is creamy.

Add the tomatoes and let the mixture cool.

Separate the crescent rolls into 2 rectangles. Press the perforations together. Spoon the chorizo mixture lengthwise down the center of each rectangle. Fold over the long sides of the rolls to cover the chorizo mixture.

Place the rolls on an ungreased baking sheet. Bake for 20 minutes or until the crust is golden.

Let cool slightly, then slice into 1½" pieces.

Serves 12

Pico de Gallo

This recipe is what you find in restaurants served with a bowl of tortilla chips for dipping. It's also a great topping for fajitas.

4 medium-size ripe tomatoes, cored, seeded, and finely diced
¼ cup minced red onion
2 jalapeño peppers, stemmed, seeded, and minced
½ cup chopped cilantro
2 tbsp. freshly squeezed lime juice
¼ tsp. salt
¼ tsp. black pepper
Tortilla chips

Combine all the ingredients in a mixing bowl. Stir to mix and let marinate for 30 minutes to blend the flavors.

Serve with tortilla chips.

Serves 8

Guacamole

There are hundreds of versions of guacamole ranging from the bland to the spicy. This recipe from my daughter, Jaime, is the best guacamole I've ever eaten. Serve with tortilla chips, on the side of a combination plate or enchilada platter, or as a topping on tacos, burgers, chicken, fajitas, or quesadillas.

4 ripe avocados
1 small tomato, peeled, seeded, diced, and drained
¼ cup finely diced onion
1 tsp. garlic salt
1 tsp. cumin
1 tsp. fajita seasoning
Juice of ½ lime
Salt to taste

Cut the avocados in half. Twist to remove from the pit. Scoop out the pulp. In a medium-size bowl, mash the avocados with a fork so that the mixture is a bit chunky.

Add the tomato, onion, garlic salt, cumin, and fajita seasoning. Mix thoroughly.

Add the lime juice and mix well. Taste and add salt and more seasonings if necessary.

Serves 12

Guacamole Cheese Chips

White tortilla chips
1½ cups shredded Monterey jack or cheddar cheese
½ cup finely diced tomatoes
1 cup guacamole

Preheat the broiler.

Arrange the tortilla chips in a single layer in a large shallow pan or on a cookie sheet.

Sprinkle the cheese and the tomatoes over the chips.

Broil until the cheese is melted.

Top with the guacamole.

Serves 12

Nachos Grande

1 lb. lean ground beef
1 large onion, chopped
1 tsp. seasoned salt
½ tsp. ground cumin
2 16 oz. cans refried beans
1 1.25 oz. package taco seasoning mix
2 cups shredded Monterey jack cheese
1 4.5 oz. can chopped green chiles
1 cup shredded cheddar cheese
¾ cup chunky picante sauce
White tortilla chips
½ cup sliced black olives
1 cup guacamole
½ cup sour cream
¼ cup chopped green onions
1 large tomato, diced

Preheat the oven to 400 degrees.

Brown the ground beef and onion in a 12" skillet over medium heat. Drain.

Add the seasoned salt and cumin. Stir to mix.

In a medium-size bowl, combine the beans, taco seasoning mix, and Monterey jack cheese. Mix well. Spread the mixture on the bottom of a 13x9" baking dish. Cover with the meat mixture.

Sprinkle the green chiles over the meat. Top with the cheddar cheese and picante sauce. Bake, uncovered, for 20 to 25 minutes or until thoroughly heated.

Arrange the chips on a plate. Spoon the meat and bean mixture over the chips. Sprinkle with the olives, guacamole, sour cream, green onions, and tomato.

Serves 12

Meaty Nachos

My daughter, Jennifer, used to make this for lunch when we lived in Chicago. She had a taste for San Antonio food years before we moved there.

1 lb. lean ground beef
1 16 oz. can refried beans
White tortilla chips
8 dashes Tabasco® sauce
1 cup shredded cheddar cheese

Brown the ground beef in a 12" skillet over medium-high heat. Drain.

Mix in the refried beans and heat through.

Arrange the chips on a plate. Spoon the meat and bean mixture over the chips. Sprinkle the Tabasco® sauce and cheddar cheese on top. Microwave just until the cheese melts.

Optional Ingredients: Add chopped tomatoes, red onions, and black olives. Serve with sour cream and mashed avocado on the side.

Serves 12

Beverages

Mexican Mocha

- 1 tbsp. ground cinnamon
- ¼ tsp. ground nutmeg
- ½ cup ground dark roast coffee
- 5 cups water
- ¼ cup firmly packed dark brown sugar
- ⅓ cup chocolate syrup
- 1 cup milk
- 1 tsp. vanilla extract
- Whipped cream
- Powdered nutmeg or cinnamon

Combine the ground cinnamon and nutmeg with the coffee grounds in a coffee filter. Add the water to the coffee maker and brew.

While the coffee is brewing, combine the brown sugar, chocolate syrup, and milk in a large saucepan. Cook over low heat, stirring constantly, until the sugar is dissolved.

Stir in the coffee mixture and the vanilla extract.

Pour into mugs. Add a dollop of whipped cream. Sprinkle with powdered nutmeg or cinnamon.

Serves 6

Cinnamon Café Latte

2 cups milk
4 4" cinnamon sticks
2 cups hot, strong coffee

Pour the milk into a saucepan. Add the cinnamon sticks and bring to a boil, stirring occasionally. Turn off the heat.

Using a slotted spoon, lift out the cinnamon sticks. While holding the cinnamon sticks above the saucepan, squeeze them with a smaller spoon to release any liquid they have absorbed. Set the cinnamon sticks aside.

Add the hot coffee to the hot milk, stir to mix, then pour into cups. Add a cinnamon stick to each cup.

Serves 4

Kahlúa Coffee

2 cups hot, strong coffee
½ cup tequila
½ cup Kahlúa
1 tsp. vanilla extract
2 tbsp. dark brown sugar
⅔ cup heavy cream

Brew the coffee in a coffee maker.

Add the tequila, Kahlúa, and vanilla extract to the coffee in the carafe. Stir well to mix.

Add the sugar and stir until it has completely dissolved.

Pour into cups. Drizzle in the cream. Serve hot.

Variation: To make **Cool Kahlúa Coffee,** place the prepared coffee in the refrigerator for 20 minutes, then pour into cups and drizzle in the cream.

Serves 4

Cinnamon Hot Chocolate

¼ cup cocoa
¼ cup sugar
½ tsp. cinnamon
¼ tsp. nutmeg
⅓ cup water
3½ cups milk
1 tsp. vanilla extract
Whipped cream
Powdered nutmeg
4 4" cinnamon sticks

Combine the cocoa, sugar, cinnamon, nutmeg, and water in a medium-size saucepan. Cook over medium heat, stirring occasionally, until the cocoa powder and sugar are dissolved.

Reduce the heat to low. Add the milk and vanilla extract. Whisk until the mixture is frothy.

Pour into mugs. Top with whipped cream and sprinkle with powdered nutmeg. Place a cinnamon stick in each mug.

Serves 4

Frozen Margaritas

This drink is popular everywhere, not just in San Antonio. It goes especially well with nachos or hot chili con queso (cheese dip) with chips while you're waiting for a table in a Tex-Mex restaurant.

3 shots tequila
1 shot triple sec
3 heaping tbsp. frozen limeade concentrate
2 cups crushed ice
Lime wedge
Coarse salt

Combine the tequila, triple sec, limeade concentrate, and crushed ice in a blender. Blend until slushy.

Frost two cocktail glasses by rubbing the outer rim with the lime wedge.

Dip each glass in a saucer of coarse salt so that it is evenly coated. Make sure that no salt goes into the glass.

Pour the frozen Margarita into the frosted glass.

Serves 2

Avocado Margarita

Fresh, light, and with a creamy kick, this Avocado Margarita, originated by Blanca Aldaco, owner of the restaurant Aldaco's, is a favorite drink in San Antonio. Aldaco's Mexican Cuisine, www.aldacos.net.

3 cups cubed ice
4 oz. Cuervo Gold Tequila
4 oz. Cointreau
2 oz. freshly squeezed lime juice
8 oz. sweet and sour, divided
2 large avocados
Chili-Lime salt*

Pour the cubed ice, tequila, Cointreau, lime juice, and 6 oz. of sweet and sour into a blender. Blend until smooth.

Slice 1 avocado in half and remove the pit. With a tablespoon, remove small portions of the pulp and place them in the blender. Do not scoop out each whole half; add it in increments so as not to overblend the frozen product so that it becomes watery.

Add remaining sweet and sour to the frozen batch and blend for about 20 seconds.

Rim two martini glasses with the Chili-Lime salt and pour in the frozen Margarita.

Slice the remaining avocado in half and remove the pit. Carefully remove each half of the pulp in 1 scoop, then cut into slices.

Gently roll the outside of the avocado slice in kosher salt or the Chili-Lime salt. Gently handle and press the inside of the avocado slice onto the rim of each glass.

Serves 2

*Chili-Lime salt is available in Latin markets. The Lucas or Trechas brands are best.

Horchata

If you have an upset stomach or a hangover, this drink will cure you. A powdered mix is sold at most of the grocery stores in town.

2¼ cups long-grain rice
3 cups water
1¼ cups blanched whole almonds
2 tsp. ground cinnamon
Finely grated zest of 1 lime
¼ cup sugar

Put the rice in a colander and rinse it thoroughly under cold running water. Drain. Transfer the rice to a large bowl and pour in the water. Cover and let soak for at least 2 hours.

Drain the rice, reserving 2½ cups of the soaking liquid. Spoon the rice into a food processor and grind very finely.

Add the almonds and process until finely ground.

Add the cinnamon, grated lime zest, and sugar. Add the reserved soaking liquid from the rice. Mix until all the sugar has dissolved.

Serve in glasses over ice.

Serves 4

Limeade

Instead of lemonade, try this refreshing drink.

7½ cups water
6 tbsp. sugar
10 limes

Pour the water into a large pitcher. Add the sugar and stir until all the sugar has dissolved. Chill for 1 hour.

Using a grater, remove the zest from the limes, being careful to take only the colored zest, not the pith. Set aside.

Squeeze the juice from the limes and add this to the chilled sugar water, along with the zest. Stir well.

Serve in glasses with ice cubes and a lime slice.

Serves 6

Helpful Hint: To extract the maximum amount of juice from the limes, roll them firmly on a countertop, pushing them with the heel of your hand.

Sangria

This homemade recipe is the best Sangria I've ever had.

2 cups rose wine
2 cups burgundy wine
1 cup orange juice
1 cup lemonade
6 tbsp. grenadine
Lemon, lime, and orange slices
Maraschino cherries

Place both wines, the orange juice, lemonade, and grenadine in a blender and blend. Serve in a wine glass over ice. Garnish with slices of lemon, lime, and orange. Top with a maraschino cherry.

Serves 6

Watermelon Aqua

This refreshing drink is perfect on those hot, sizzling summer days.

8 cups cubed, seeded watermelon, about 1 6 lb. watermelon
1 cup water
½ cup sugar
¼ cup fresh lime juice
4 cups club soda, chilled
Lime slices

Combine half the watermelon, half the water, and half the sugar in a blender. Blend until smooth.

Strain into a large container. Repeat with the remaining watermelon, water, and sugar.

Stir in the lime juice. Refrigerate until well chilled, about 4 hours.

When ready to serve, stir in the club soda. Garnish the glasses with a lime slice.

Serves 12

Tequila Sunrise

While I wouldn't recommend starting your day off with tequila, this drink will certainly open your eyes.

1½ tbsp. tequila
¼ cup freshly squeezed orange juice
Juice of 1 lime
1 tsp. grenadine

Pour the tequila into a cocktail glass, then add the orange and lime juices. Stir gently to mix.

Add the grenadine, pouring it in a swirling pattern slowly down the back of a spoon held over the glass.

Serves 1

Breakfast

Huevos Rancheros

Huevos Rancheros means eggs and sauce. This is a favorite way to start the day, San Antonio style. There are dozens of recipes for Huevos Rancheros, but this one is quick and easy.

2 cups cubed tomatoes
1 to 2 tbsp. butter
¼ cup finely chopped onion
1 serrano pepper, stemmed, seeded, and minced
1 garlic clove, minced
Salt to taste
Vegetable cooking spray
6 6" corn tortillas
2 to 3 tbsp. butter
6 large eggs
Salt and black pepper to taste

Put the tomatoes in a food processor or a blender and process until almost smooth.

Heat the butter in a 12" skillet over medium heat. When it sizzles, add the onion, serrano pepper, and garlic. Sauté until tender, about 3 to 4 minutes.

Add the tomatoes and heat to boiling. Continue to cook over medium heat, stirring occasionally, until the mixture thickens, about 5 to 8 minutes. Season to taste with salt.

While this is cooking, spray both sides of the tortillas lightly with cooking spray. Cook in a separate 12" skillet over medium heat until browned, about 1 minute on each side. Place on serving plates and set aside.

Add the butter to the skillet. When it sizzles, add the eggs and fry. Season to taste with salt and black pepper. Place on top of the tortillas. Spoon the sauce over.

Serves 6

Chipotle-Bean Huevos Rancheros

1 small avocado
⅓ cup freshly chopped cilantro
⅓ cup minced green onions
1½ tbsp. freshly squeezed lime juice
Salt and black pepper to taste
Nonstick cooking spray
4 6" corn tortillas
4 tsp. vegetable oil, divided
1 cup finely chopped onion
3 garlic cloves, minced
1½ tsp. ground cumin
1 28 oz. can diced tomatoes, with juice
1 15 oz. can black beans, drained and rinsed
2 tsp. chopped canned chipotle chiles
4 large eggs
Salt and black pepper to taste
½ cup grated cheddar cheese
2 cups chopped romaine lettuce

Scoop out the pulp of the avocado into a medium-size bowl. Add the cilantro and green onions. Squeeze the lime juice over and stir to mix. Season to taste with salt and black pepper. Set aside.

Preheat the oven to 400 degrees. Lightly spray a large baking sheet with nonstick cooking spray. Arrange the tortillas in a single layer on the baking sheet. Bake for 15 minutes or until the tortillas are golden.

While the tortillas are cooking, heat 3 tsp. of the vegetable oil in a 12" nonstick skillet over medium-high heat. Add the onion and sauté until golden, about 5 minutes.

Add the garlic and cumin; stir briefly to mix.

Add the tomatoes with juice, beans, and chipotle chiles. Bring to a boil, then reduce the heat to low and simmer for 10 minutes or until almost all of the liquid is absorbed, stirring frequently.

In another 12" nonstick skillet, heat the remaining 1 tsp. vegetable oil over medium heat. Crack the eggs into the skillet and cook until the whites are set but the yolks are still soft. Sprinkle with salt and pepper to taste.

Place the warm tortillas on four plates. Divide the bean mixture among the tortillas. Top each with an egg, then sprinkle with the cheese and the lettuce. Top with the avocado mixture.

Serves 4

Breakfast Tacos

San Antonians start their morning with a breakfast of eggs, salsa, and cheese, all wrapped together in fresh, warm tortillas. The annual taco breakfast, also called the Cowboy Breakfast, which is held in February to kick off the rodeo, draws thousands of hungry people for a free taco or a sausage biscuit with gravy.

¼ lb. chorizo sausage
½ cup chopped onion
1½ cups diced, boiled potatoes
3 large eggs
½ cup milk
6 8" flour tortillas, warmed
½ cup salsa, warmed
1 cup shredded Monterey jack cheese

Cook the chorizo and onion in a 12" skillet over medium heat. Drain.

Add the diced potatoes to the skillet. Cook for 3 to 4 minutes to brown on all sides.

Beat the eggs together with the milk in a medium-size mixing bowl. Pour into the skillet. Cook, stirring, until the eggs are set.

Spoon the mixture into the warmed tortillas. Top with salsa and cheese. Fold the tortillas in half or roll them, tucking in the sides, and enjoy your hand-held breakfast.

Serves 6

Optional: Spread some warmed refried beans on the tortillas before adding the ingredients.

Alamo Eggs

A great way to start the day, sunny side up. The spicy chorizo and ranchero sauce will definitely open your eyes and wake you up.

¼ lb. chorizo sausage
1 cup Ranchero Sauce (see page 219)
½ cup grated Mexican Blend cheese
2 tbsp. butter
4 large eggs
4 6" corn tortillas

Cook the chorizo in a 12" skillet over medium-high heat. Drain.

Add the Ranchero Sauce and heat to boiling, stirring.

Reduce the heat to low. Add the cheese and stir to mix until the cheese melts. Remove the pan from the heat.

Melt the butter in a separate 12" skillet. Add the eggs and cook sunny side up or over easy.

Wrap the tortillas in plastic wrap and microwave for 15 to 20 seconds to warm them.

Dip the warmed tortillas in the chorizo-ranchero sauce. Place 2 tortillas on each plate. Top with the eggs and the remaining sauce.

Serves 2

Chorizo Scrambled Eggs

This breakfast is great as is, but you can make it even better by making it into a breakfast burrito. Spread warmed tortillas with mashed avocado or refried beans and top the eggs with fresh salsa and a sprinkling of grated cheese. Wrap it all up and enjoy.

½ lb. chorizo sausage
1 medium onion, chopped
10 large eggs
¼ cup milk
¼ cup cilantro leaves, chopped
3 green onions, trimmed and sliced
1½ cups grated Mexican Blend cheese
6 10" flour tortillas, warmed
1 medium tomato, coarsely chopped

Cook the chorizo and onion in a 12" skillet over medium-high heat until browned, about 10 minutes. Drain.

Reduce the heat to medium low. In a medium-size bowl, beat the eggs with the milk until frothy, then pour into the pan. Stir to scramble until soft set.

Stir in the cilantro and green onions just before the eggs are set. Top with cheese.

Serve with warm tortillas and the chopped tomato on the side.

Serves 6

Easy Salsa Omelet

This omelet is a quick and easy breakfast. Enjoy by itself or with a fresh, warm flour tortilla.

1 tbsp. butter
2 tbsp. chopped onion
1 large egg beaten with 2 tbsp. milk
¼ cup shredded cheddar cheese, divided
4 tbsp. chunky salsa

Melt the butter in an 8" skillet over medium heat. Add the onion and sauté for 1 to 2 minutes or until translucent.

Pour in the egg mixture. Cook for 2 to 3 minutes, or until the sides and center are set, then flip the omelet over with a spatula. Sprinkle a handful of the cheddar cheese on top.

Cook for 1 to 2 minutes on the second side, then fold the omelet in half. Remove to a plate.

Put the salsa in the skillet and stir with a spatula to warm. Top the omelet with the hot salsa and sprinkle the remaining cheese on top.

Serves 1

Eggs Olé

This breakfast is a bright beginning for a sun-filled San Antonio day. Serve the eggs alone or wrap them in a warm flour tortilla and top with salsa.

2 tbsp. butter
3 tbsp. onion, diced
3 tbsp. green bell pepper, diced
1 small garlic clove, minced
4 tbsp. jalapeño pepper, chopped
1 roma tomato, chopped
¼ tsp. chili powder
2 large eggs beaten with 2 tbsp. milk
Salt and black pepper to taste

Melt the butter in a 10" skillet over medium heat. Add the onion and the green bell pepper. Sauté until the onion and bell pepper have softened, about 5 minutes.

Reduce the heat to medium low. Add the garlic, jalapeño pepper, tomato, and chili powder. Cook for 2 minutes, stirring.

Add the eggs; stir to scramble. Season to taste with salt and pepper.

Serves 1

Variation: To make **Cheesy Eggs Olé**, top with a handful of shredded cheddar cheese.

Poblano Hash and Eggs

- 2 to 3 tbsp. butter
- 1½ cups chopped poblano peppers
- ½ cup chopped onion
- 2 cups cubed, peeled, cooked potatoes
- Salt and black pepper to taste
- 4 large eggs
- Fresh cilantro sprigs
- ½ cup salsa, warmed

Melt the butter in a large skillet. When it sizzles, add the poblano peppers and onion. Sauté for about 5 minutes or until softened.

Add the potatoes and cook until the potatoes are browned, about 5 to 8 more minutes. Season to taste with salt and pepper.

While this is cooking, fry or poach the eggs.

Place the poblano-potato mixture on individual plates and top each with an egg. Place a cilantro sprig on the side. Serve with salsa.

Serves 4

Salsa Scrambled Eggs

- 4 taco shells
- ⅔ cup salsa
- ½ cup black beans, drained and rinsed
- 5 tbsp. freshly chopped cilantro, divided
- 2 tbsp. butter
- 5 large eggs
- 1 tbsp. milk
- Salt and black pepper to taste
- 3 tbsp. cream cheese, diced

Preheat the oven to 250 degrees. Place the taco shells on a baking sheet and warm in the oven for 10 minutes.

Stir together the salsa, beans, and 3 tbsp. cilantro in a medium bowl. Set aside.

Melt the butter in a 10" skillet over medium-low heat.

Whisk the eggs, the remaining 2 tbsp. cilantro, and milk in a medium-size bowl. Season to taste with salt and black pepper.

Pour the egg mixture into the skillet. Add the cream cheese pieces. Cook, stirring, until the eggs are creamy.

Spoon the eggs into the warmed taco shells. Top with the salsa mixture.

Serves 4

Serrano Omelet

This breakfast will open your eyes and get you going in the morning. Roasting the peppers gives them added depth and flavor.

4 tbsp. butter, divided
½ cup diced tomatoes
3 tbsp. chopped onion
2 large eggs beaten with 2 tbsp. milk
1 to 2 serrano peppers, roasted, peeled, seeded, and diced
¼ cup grated Monterey jack cheese

Melt half the butter in an 8" skillet over medium heat. Add the tomatoes and onion. Cook for 2 to 3 minutes, or until the onion is tender. Remove and set aside. Drain any juices from the skillet and add them to the tomato-onion mixture.

Place the remaining butter in the same skillet. When the butter has melted and begun to sizzle, add the eggs and cook on the first side for 1 to 2 minutes, or until the top is set and the bottom is lightly golden.

Using a spatula, carefully flip the omelet over. Sprinkle the serrano peppers and cheese over the top. Add half of the tomato-onion mixture. Cook for 1 to 2 more minutes, then fold the omelet in half.

Serve the omelet topped with the remaining tomatoes and onion.

Serves 1

Note: There are two ways to roast peppers. Either char them under the broiler or place them in a skillet and dry roast them. Peel off the charred skin and you're good to go.

Sunny-Side Eggs

Tostadas are crispy corn tortillas. They are available in grocery stores right alongside other types of tortillas.

½ lb. chorizo sausage
1 15 oz. can refried black beans
3 tbsp. olive oil, divided
1 medium onion, chopped
4 6" tostadas
4 large eggs
½ cup salsa, warmed
1 avocado, diced
½ cup Monterey jack cheese

Preheat the oven to 300 degrees.

Cook the chorizo in a 12" skillet over medium-high heat. Drain.

Add the beans to the chorizo in the skillet and stir until heated through. Remove the pan from the heat and cover to keep warm.

Heat 1 tbsp. oil in another 12" nonstick skillet over medium-high heat. Add the onion and sauté until soft.

Arrange the tostadas on a baking sheet. Spread ⅓ cup of the bean-chorizo mixture on each tostada. Top with the onion. Place in the oven to keep warm.

Heat the remaining 2 tbsp. oil in the same skillet over medium-high heat. Add the eggs, one at a time, and cook sunny side up until done.

Remove the tostadas from the oven and place one egg on each. Top with the salsa, avocado, and cheese.

Serves 4

Breakfast Bake

This makes a great brunch for a lazy San Antonio Sunday. You can make this the night before and just pop it into the oven while you lounge around.

½ lb. chorizo sausage
8 large eggs
1 10¾ oz. can cream of mushroom soup
½ cup chopped green onions
1½ cups shredded cheddar cheese
½ cup chunky salsa
½ cup sour cream
1 4.5 oz. can roasted green chiles, drained, rinsed, and chopped
12 corn tortillas, torn into 1" wide strips
1 cup shredded Monterey jack cheese

Cook the chorizo sausage in a 10" skillet over medium heat. Drain.

Lightly coat a 13x9" baking dish with nonstick cooking spray. Set aside.

Beat the eggs together in a large mixing bowl. Add the soup and whisk until the mixture is smooth.

Add the cooked sausage, onions, cheddar cheese, salsa, sour cream, chiles, and tortillas. Stir until blended.

Pour the mixture into the prepared dish. Sprinkle the Monterey jack cheese on top. Refrigerate, covered, 4 to 24 hours.

When ready to cook, preheat the oven to 350 degrees. Bring the casserole to room temperature, then bake for 45 minutes or until the top is brown and the eggs are set. Let rest 5 minutes before cutting.

Serves 4

Breakfast Chile Relleno

Served outside on the patio, this makes a great brunch on a lazy Saturday morning.

8 poblano peppers, roasted, peeled, and deveined, divided
½ cup milk
1 tsp. salt
1 to 2 tbsp. vegetable oil
2 large garlic cloves, minced
½ onion, very finely sliced into slivers
1 cup heavy cream
12 medium-size eggs
6 oz. thinly sliced smoked ham, cut into small pieces
2 green onions, finely cut from end to end, both the white and green parts
2 serrano peppers, stemmed, seeded, and finely chopped
Salt to taste
3 tbsp. vegetable oil
12 oz. shredded Monterey jack cheese
1 medium tomato, diced (optional)

To roast the poblano peppers, put olive oil on your fingertips and rub the oil over the poblanos evenly. Place them on a hot comal (skillet), on a grill, or under a broiler, turning as needed until the skin is evenly charred. Place them on a plate and cover with a damp towel to allow the peppers to steam for about 10 minutes. When cool enough to handle, remove the charred skin. Hold the pepper from the stem and cut 6 of them with a 1" slit across and a 2" slit down (as in a 'T'). Open gently and remove the veins and seeds. For the remaining 2 poblanos, simply remove the stems, seeds, and veins.

To make the poblano sauce, place the 2 peppers without the slits in a blender, along with the milk and 1 tsp. salt. Blend until smooth. Set aside.

Heat 1 to 2 tbsp. vegetable oil in a saucepan over medium-high heat. Add the garlic and slivered onion. Sauté until translucent, about 5 to 7 minutes.

Add the heavy cream and the poblano purée. Reduce the heat and let simmer for 2 to 3 minutes until the flavors blend. Remove the pan from the heat and set aside.

In a medium-size bowl, combine the eggs with the ham, green onions, serrano peppers, and salt to taste. Stir briskly to mix.

Heat 3 tbsp. vegetable oil in a 12" skillet over medium heat. Add the egg mixture and cook, stirring. (It's better to undercook the eggs at this point, since they will be cooked further in the oven.)

Preheat the oven to 350 degrees. Lightly spray a 13x9" glass baking dish with cooking spray.

Place a poblano in your palm with the slit facing you. Open gently, then place a few tbsp. of the cheese along the bottom. Add some of the scrambled egg mixture, then more cheese. With both hands, firmly reshape the poblano and place on the prepared baking dish. Repeat with the other 5 poblanos.

Pour the poblano sauce over the top. Bake for 13 to 15 minutes or until heated through.

Garnish with the fresh diced tomatoes.

Serves 4

Fredericksburg French Toast

Fredericksburg (www.fredericksburg-texas.com) is about an hour's drive from San Antonio. Filled with quaint antique shops and German boutiques, the city is famous for its peaches as well as several wineries.

3 fresh peaches, peeled and pitted
2 tbsp. chopped pecans
1 3 oz. package cream cheese, softened
12 slices country bread
2 large eggs
½ cup milk
½ tsp. ground cinnamon
¼ tsp. vanilla extract
4 tbsp. butter, divided

Chop 1 peach and slice the other 2. Place the chopped peach in a small bowl. Set the sliced peaches aside.

Add the pecans and cream cheese to the chopped peach and stir to mix.

Spoon 1½ tbsp. of the cream cheese mixture onto each of 6 bread slices, spreading evenly. Top with the remaining slices of bread.

In a small bowl, beat together the eggs, milk, cinnamon, and vanilla extract. Dip each sandwich into this mixture, turning to coat both sides.

Melt 1 tbsp. of the butter over medium heat in a 12" skillet or griddle. Cook 2 sandwiches at a time for 3 minutes on each side, adding more butter as needed.

Serve topped with the remaining peach slices.

Serves 6

Chorizo Quiche

2 8" corn tortillas, cut into 1" strips
¼ cup all-purpose flour
¾ tsp. chili powder
½ tsp. salt
1 medium tomato, chopped
⅓ cup salsa
3 green onions, chopped
1 jalapeño pepper, seeded and minced
¼ lb. chorizo sausage, cooked and crumbled
5 large eggs
¾ cup milk
½ 10 oz. package frozen chopped spinach, thawed and squeezed dry
1 cup grated Monterey jack cheese, divided

Preheat the oven to 350 degrees. Lightly butter the bottom of a 9" pie pan. Place the tortilla strips in the bottom of the pan, slightly overlapping them.

In a small bowl, combine the flour, chili powder, and salt. Sprinkle half of this mixture over the tortilla strips.

In a medium-size bowl, combine the tomato, salsa, green onions, and jalapeño. Layer this over the flour mixture.

Sprinkle the remaining flour mixture on top of the tomato mixture. Sprinkle the cooked chorizo on top of the flour mixture.

In a medium-size bowl, whisk the eggs and milk together. Add the spinach and half of the cheese. Stir to mix. Pour evenly over the top. Bake, uncovered, for 30 minutes.

Remove from the oven and sprinkle with the remaining cheese. Return to the oven and bake for 5 more minutes. Let rest for 5 minutes before cutting.

Serves 6

Salads

Grilled Chicken Strip Salad

This is a great salad to enjoy on one of those hot, sultry San Antonio nights.

4 cups coarsely chopped mixed salad greens
1 6 oz. package precooked, Southwest-seasoned chicken breast strips
1 cup coarsely shredded cheddar cheese
2 tomatoes, each cut into 8 wedges
1 avocado, coarsely mashed
1 tbsp. chili powder
2 tsp. garlic powder
½ 15 oz. can black beans, drained and rinsed
½ cup sliced green onions
¼ cup sliced black olives
Ranch dressing

To serve family style, arrange the salad greens on a large serving platter. Top with all the remaining ingredients except the dressing. Serve the dressing on the side.

Serves 4

Variation / Optional Additions: Crush tortilla chips or Doritos® and sprinkle on top of the salad. To make a **Grilled Chicken Wrap,** wrap individual portions of all the ingredients in warmed flour tortillas. Top with salsa instead of ranch dressing.

Chicken Tostada Salad

Salads in San Antonio are usually eaten on top of a crisp tostada, layered with beans, cheese, meat, lettuce, tomato, onions, and, of course, avocado.

3 boneless, skinless chicken breasts, cooked and shredded
4 green onions, chopped
½ cup chopped cilantro
4 cups iceberg lettuce, shredded
1 large tomato, seeded and diced
½ cup shredded Mexican Blend cheese*
¼ cup red wine vinegar
¾ cup olive oil
Salt and black pepper to taste
1 cup refried beans
8 prepared tostada shells
8 tbsp. sour cream
2 avocados, peeled, pitted, and thinly sliced

Combine the chicken, onions, and cilantro in a medium-size bowl.

Combine the lettuce, tomato, and cheese in another medium-size bowl.

Combine the red wine vinegar, olive oil, salt, and black pepper in a small jar or bottle. Cover and shake vigorously to combine or whisk the ingredients together in a bowl.

Heat the beans in the microwave or in a small saucepan over low heat, stirring often to prevent sticking. Add some water if necessary.

Spread a thin layer of beans on each tostada shell. Spoon the sour cream over. Top with the avocado slices.

Pour enough of the dressing on the chicken mixture to coat it generously, then toss well. Scatter the chicken mixture over the avocado slices.

Toss the remaining dressing with the lettuce mixture, then cover the chicken mixture with it.

Serves 8

Note: If you can't find tostada shells, substitute 8 6" corn tortillas. Fry them in vegetable oil until crisp, then drain on paper towels.

Substitutions: Use cooked pork, chorizo sausage, or ground beef instead of chicken.

* Mexican Blend cheese, also called Fiesta cheese, is a combination of four shredded cheeses: cheddar, Monterey jack, asadero, and queso blanco. This blend is sold in all grocery stores.

Pico Chicken Salad

I first enjoyed this salad at EZ's Brick Oven & Grill restaurant. This is my version.

1 8.75 oz. can corn, drained
½ 15 oz. can black beans, rinsed and drained
1 cup dry rotini noodles
4 cups chopped romaine lettuce
1 6 oz. package precooked, Southwest-seasoned chicken breast strips
1 large tomato, chopped
Balsamic dressing
1 cup shredded Parmesan cheese

Cook the corn and black beans with the rotini (corkscrew) noodles for 10 minutes or until the pasta is cooked. Drain in a colander and rinse under cold water until the pasta is cooled.

Place the lettuce in a large serving bowl. Add the chicken strips, tomato, and cooled pasta mixture. Toss with balsamic dressing and sprinkle with Parmesan cheese.

Serves 4

South of the Border Salad

This can be either a salad or a wrap.

1 lb. lean ground beef
2 tbsp. or more chili powder to taste
1 1.25 oz. package taco seasoning mix
½ cup water
White tortilla chips
6 cups lettuce, cut into ribbons
½ cup shredded cheddar cheese
½ cup shredded Monterey jack cheese
1 8 oz. container sour cream
½ avocado, mashed
1 medium tomato, chopped

Brown the ground beef in a 12" skillet over medium heat. Drain. Add the chili powder to coat the meat. Stir in the taco mix and water. Heat to boiling, stirring. Reduce the heat and simmer for 10 minutes, stirring occasionally.

While this is cooking, spread the tortilla chips in a baking pan. Warm the chips in the oven at 200 degrees for 5 minutes.

Arrange the lettuce and tortilla chips on individual plates. Spoon the hot meat mixture over the chips. Top with cheeses, sour cream, mashed avocado, and tomato.

If you'd prefer sandwiches instead of a salad, use 4 8" flour tortillas, warmed in a skillet or in the microwave. Use only 1 cup lettuce, shredded. Place all the ingredients in the tortilla and wrap.

Serves 4

Variation: To make a **South of the Border Chicken Salad**, use 2 cups chopped, shredded chicken instead of ground beef. Add ¼ cup pitted black olives, sliced, and ½ cup dark red kidney beans, drained and rinsed.

Terrific Taco Cups

Instead of serving this salad in a bowl, it's served in taco cups.

1 lb. lean ground beef
1 large green bell pepper, chopped
3 garlic cloves, minced
1 15.5 oz. can red kidney beans, drained and rinsed
1 8 oz. jar taco sauce
¾ cup fresh or frozen corn
1 tbsp. chili powder
8 cups torn lettuce
2 medium tomatoes, chopped
1 cup shredded cheddar cheese, divided
4 green onions, chopped
6 tortilla cups*
1 cup guacamole

Cook the ground beef, green bell pepper, and garlic in a 12" skillet over medium heat. Drain.

Stir in the beans, taco sauce, corn, and chili powder. Bring to a boil, then reduce the heat, cover, and simmer for 10 minutes.

Combine the lettuce, tomatoes, ¾ cup cheese, and green onions in a large bowl.

Divide the lettuce mixture among the tortilla cups.

Spoon equal amounts of the beef mixture into each cup. Top with guacamole and remaining cheese.

Serves 6

*Tortilla cups are shaped like a bowl with waves, similar to large paper muffin cups. You can find them in the bread section in your local grocery store.

Doritos® Dish

1 lb. lean ground beef
¼ tsp. chili powder
¼ tsp. garlic powder
1 15.5 oz. can red kidney beans, drained and rinsed
½ head iceberg lettuce, chopped
4 medium tomatoes, chopped
2 green onions, chopped
1 cup grated cheddar cheese
2 cups crushed Doritos® chips
¾ cup Ranch dressing

Brown the ground beef in a 12" skillet over medium heat. Drain, then add chili powder and garlic powder. Stir to coat the meat.

Add beans and heat through.

Place the lettuce, tomatoes, onions, and cheese in a large serving bowl. Add the meat mixture. Mix in the chips. Toss with ranch dressing.

Serves 4

Soups and Stews

Black Bean Potato Soup

¾ cup chopped onion
2 tsp. minced garlic
¼ tsp. dried oregano
1½ tsp. cumin
1½ cups water
2 beef bouillon cubes
2 small red potatoes, chopped with skin on
4 to 5 fresh spinach leaves, washed and chopped
2 15 oz. cans black beans, drained and rinsed
1 cup crushed Fritos®
1 cup grated cheddar cheese

Combine the onion, garlic, oregano, cumin, water, bouillon cubes, potatoes, spinach, and black beans in a medium-size saucepan. Bring to a boil, then reduce the heat, cover, and simmer for 30 minutes, stirring occasionally.

Ladle into individual serving bowls. Sprinkle the soup with crushed Fritos® and grated cheddar cheese just before serving.

Serves 4

Black Bean Soup

10 strips bacon, chopped
1 red bell pepper, chopped
1 small onion, chopped
3 carrots, chopped
2 garlic cloves, chopped
2 cups chicken broth
1¼ cups water
2 15 oz. cans black beans, drained and rinsed
2 tbsp. finely chopped cilantro
1 tbsp. lemon juice
1 tsp. dried oregano
½ tsp. dried thyme
¼ tsp. crushed red pepper
¼ jalapeño pepper, finely chopped
⅛ tsp. black pepper
1 tomato, diced
1 8 oz. container sour cream

Cook the bacon, along with the bell pepper, onion, carrots, and garlic in a large saucepan over medium heat until the bacon is crisp and the vegetables have softened. Drain.

Stir in the broth, water, beans, cilantro, lemon juice, oregano, thyme, crushed red pepper, jalapeño, and black pepper. Bring to a boil, then reduce the heat and simmer, covered, for 10 minutes.

Ladle into individual soup bowls. Top with the diced tomato and a dollop of sour cream.

Serves 4

Black-Eyed Pea Soup

Black-eyed pea soup is a favorite at many Tex-Mex restaurants. Omit the chorizo and the tomato juice and you have a vegetable side dish.

2 to 3 tbsp. olive oil
1 red bell pepper, chopped
1 medium onion, chopped
2 garlic cloves, finely chopped
2 stalks celery, chopped
3 15.5 oz. cans black-eyed peas, drained and rinsed
1 lb. chorizo sausage, cooked and drained
1 11 oz. can tomato juice
1 10 oz. can diced tomatoes and chiles, with juice

Heat the oil in a large saucepan over medium heat. Add the bell pepper, onion, garlic, and celery. Sauté until tender.

Add the black-eyed peas, cooked chorizo, tomato juice, and tomatoes. Bring to a boil, then reduce the heat, cover, and simmer for 45 minutes, stirring occasionally.

Serves 4

Note: For a less spicy soup, substitute 3 cups diced, cooked ham for the chorizo.

Chicken Tortilla Soup

Tortilla soup is on the menu at most San Antonio restaurants. There are many versions of this recipe, with the constant ingredient being tortilla strips. The strips are usually fried, but this recipe cuts the fat by baking them in the oven.

3 skinless, boneless chicken breasts
3½ cups chicken broth
1 tbsp. butter
1 small onion, chopped
1 garlic clove, minced
½ tsp. ground cumin
1 14.5 oz. can diced tomatoes, with juice
1 8 oz. can tomato sauce
1 4 oz. can whole green chile peppers, rinsed, seeded, and cut into thin strips
¼ cup snipped cilantro
1 tsp. dried oregano
6 6" corn tortillas
½ cup shredded Monterey jack cheese
½ cup shredded cheddar cheese

Combine the chicken and broth in a large saucepan. Bring to a boil, then reduce the heat, cover, and simmer for 15 minutes or until the chicken is cooked through and tender. Remove the pan from the heat. Remove the chicken to a plate. When cool, shred with two forks and set aside. Skim the fat from the broth and reserve the broth.

While the chicken is cooling, melt the butter in a 10" skillet over medium heat. Add the onion, garlic, and cumin. Sauté until the onion is tender.

Preheat the oven to 350 degrees.

Stir the onion mixture into the reserved broth. Add the tomatoes, tomato sauce, chile peppers, cilantro, and oregano. Bring to a boil, then reduce the heat, cover, and simmer for 20 minutes.

While the soup is cooking, cut the tortillas in half, then cut them crosswise into ½" wide strips. Place the cut tortillas on a cookie sheet, lightly spray both sides with cooking spray, and bake for 4 to 5 minutes or until crisp.

While the tortilla strips are baking, stir the shredded chicken into the soup and heat through.

Divide the tortilla strips among the soup bowls. Ladle the soup over the strips. Top with the shredded cheeses.

Serves 4

Chicken Chiles 'n' Corn Soup

This delicious soup, simmering on the stovetop, will fill your home with a wonderful aroma.

3 tbsp. cornstarch
3 tbsp. cold water
4 cups chopped chicken
1 15 oz. can whole corn
3 10 oz. cans chicken broth
1 8 oz. can tomato sauce
2 10 oz. cans diced tomatoes with green chiles
1 medium onion, chopped
1 tsp. garlic powder
1 tsp. dried oregano

Mix the cornstarch and water together in a small bowl to form a paste. This will thicken the soup as it cooks.

Combine all the ingredients in a Dutch oven. Stir to mix well. Bring to a boil, then reduce the heat, cover, and simmer for 2 hours, stirring occasionally.

Serves 4

Chicken Pinto Soup

Start this soup the night before. If you plan to have it for dinner instead of lunch, cook it on low heat in a crockpot for 7 hours.

1 32 oz. package dried pinto beans
2 to 3 tbsp. olive oil
3 skinless, boneless chicken breasts, chopped
2 14.5 oz. cans Mexican-style tomatoes, with juice
1 15 oz. can whole kernel corn, drained
2 1.25 oz. packages taco seasoning mix
½ cup lemon juice
1 medium onion, chopped
1 8 oz. container sour cream

Rinse the beans and soak them overnight.

Heat the olive oil in a large saucepan over medium-high heat. Add the chopped chicken and brown it on all sides.

While the chicken is cooking, drain and rinse the beans in a colander. Add the beans to the chicken in the saucepan and cover with water.

Add the tomatoes, corn, taco seasoning, lemon juice, and onion. Bring to a boil, then reduce the heat and simmer for 1 hour or until the beans are tender.

Ladle into individual soup bowls. Top with a dollop of sour cream.

Serves 4

Shredded Chicken Tomatillo Soup

6 cups chicken broth
3 skinless, boneless chicken breasts
2 tbsp. vegetable oil
1 medium onion, thinly sliced
¼ tsp. salt
½ tsp. black pepper
3 garlic cloves, crushed
1 16 oz. jar green tomatillo salsa
½ bunch cilantro leaves, chopped
36 white tortilla chips
¼ cup shredded Mexican Blend cheese
½ cup diced green onions
½ cup sour cream

Bring the broth to a boil in a medium saucepan. Reduce the heat, add the chicken and simmer, covered, for 10 minutes to poach.

Remove the chicken, reserving the broth in the pan. Let the chicken cool, then shred into long strips using two forks.

Heat the oil in a Dutch oven over medium heat. Add the onion, sprinkle with salt and pepper, and sauté until the onion is tender.

Add the garlic and sauté for 2 minutes.

Add the salsa and bring to a boil. Reduce the heat and pour in the reserved chicken broth. Simmer for 10 minutes.

Add the shredded chicken. Bring to a boil, then stir in the cilantro and tortilla chips. Reduce the heat and simmer for 5 more minutes.

Ladle into individual soup bowls. Top with the cheese, green onions, and a dollop of sour cream.

Serves 4

Variation: To make **Tomatillo Pork Stew**, substitute 1½ lb. pork butt, trimmed of fat and cut into cubes, for the chicken. Decrease the chicken broth to 4 cups.

Creamy Salsa Soup

This quick and easy soup is great when you're short on time. It's the San Antonio version of tomato soup.

2 cups ready-made salsa
2 cups half-and-half
1 cup grated Monterey jack cheese
½ cup chopped green onions
Tortilla chips

Place the salsa, half-and-half, and cheese in a large saucepan. Simmer gently until heated through, stirring occasionally.

Ladle into individual soup bowls. Top with the green onions. Serve with tortilla chips.

Serves 4

Easy Enchilada Soup

If you prefer your enchiladas in a bowl rather than on a plate, you'll enjoy this soup.

1 lb. lean ground beef
⅓ cup chopped onion
½ cup chopped red bell pepper
1 4.5 oz. can chopped green chiles, drained and rinsed
1 tsp. chili powder
½ tsp. ground cumin
1 8 oz. can tomato sauce
1 cup beef broth
6 corn tortillas, cut into ½" pieces
1 cup sour cream
1 cup shredded cheddar cheese

Brown the ground beef with the onion and red bell pepper in a large saucepan over medium heat.

Add the chiles, chili powder, and cumin. Stir constantly for 2 minutes.

Add the tomato sauce and the beef broth. Stir to mix thoroughly.

Remove the pan from the heat. Add the tortilla pieces, sour cream, and cheese. Stir until the cheese is melted.

Ladle into individual soup bowls.

Serves 4

Variation: To make **Chicken Enchilada Soup**, use 2 skinless, boneless chicken breasts, coarsely chopped, instead of the ground beef. Brown the chicken in 2 tsp. olive oil, along with the onion and red bell pepper. Add the tomato sauce. Substitute chicken broth for the beef broth. Simmer for 10 minutes or until the chicken is cooked through and tender. Follow the remainder of the recipe.

Slow Picante Soup

Just toss all the ingredients into a slow cooker and dinner will be ready when you get home. Serve with cornbread.

- 2 lb. stew beef
- 1 14.5 oz. can Mexican tomatoes, with juice
- 1 10.5 oz. can beef broth
- 1 8 oz. jar picante sauce
- 1 10 oz. bag frozen corn, thawed
- 1 garlic clove, minced
- ½ tsp. ground cumin
- ½ tsp. salt
- ½ tsp. black pepper

Rinse the beef with water and place into a 12" skillet. Brown the beef on all sides over medium-high heat. Add water if necessary.

Place the beef, with any juices, along with the tomatoes, broth, picante sauce, corn, garlic, cumin, salt, and pepper in a crockpot. Stir to mix. Cook on high for 3 to 4 hours or on low for 6 to 8 hours.

Serves 4

Smoked Mesquite Turkey Soup

Mesquite turkey adds an authentic flavor to this soup. You can buy it precooked at the deli. Ask them to slice it thickly.

2 14.5 oz. cans Mexican-style tomatoes, with juice
1 14.5 oz. can chicken broth
1 lb. mesquite smoked turkey, cubed
1 large green bell pepper, chopped
1 8 oz. can whole kernel corn, drained
¾ cup picante sauce or salsa
1 2.5 oz. can sliced black olives, drained
1½ tsp. ground cumin
1 tsp. dried basil
1 garlic clove, crushed
½ cup sliced green onions
1 8 oz. container sour cream
1 cup shredded Monterey jack cheese
¼ cup chopped cilantro

In a large saucepan, combine the tomatoes, broth, turkey, green bell pepper, corn, picante sauce, olives, cumin, basil, and garlic. Bring to a boil, then reduce the heat and simmer for 10 minutes, uncovered, stirring occasionally or until the bell pepper is soft.

Add the green onions and simmer for 5 more minutes.

Ladle into individual soup bowls. Top each with sour cream, cheese, and cilantro.

Serves 4

Green Chile Pork Stew

1 lb. boneless pork tenderloin, cut into 1½" cubes
1 medium onion, chopped
3 celery stalks, chopped
2 medium carrots, chopped
2 medium unpeeled red potatoes, cubed
1 7 oz. can diced green chiles
2 tsp. chopped garlic
1 cup chicken broth
1 cup water, or enough to cover
2 tbsp. cornstarch
¼ cup water
Salt and black pepper to taste
Freshly chopped cilantro
Cornbread and butter

Mix the pork with the onion, celery, carrots, potatoes, green chiles, garlic, and chicken broth in a large saucepan. Add the water. Cover and simmer for 45 minutes.

In a small bowl, mix the cornstarch with ¼ cup water until it forms a smooth paste.

Add the cornstarch mixture to the stew to thicken. Increase the heat and stir until bubbly and the stew has thickened. Season with salt and pepper to taste.

Ladle into individual serving bowls. Sprinkle with the chopped cilantro. Serve with warm, buttered cornbread.

Serves 4

Veggies, Beans, and Rice

Baked Zucchini Boats

6 medium zucchini
1 10 oz. can diced tomatoes with chiles, divided
¼ cup grated cheddar cheese
1 tbsp. fresh lemon juice
½ tsp. garlic powder
½ tsp. dried oregano
½ 8 oz. package shredded Mexican Blend cheese
Freshly chopped cilantro

Preheat the oven to 350 degrees.

Cut the zucchini in half lengthwise and carefully scoop out the pulp with a spoon, making sure not to tear the zucchini shells. Reserve the pulp.

In a medium-size mixing bowl, combine half of the tomatoes, the reserved pulp, cheddar cheese, lemon juice, garlic powder, and oregano.

Fill the zucchini shells with this mixture, mounding slightly.

Place the zucchini "boats" in a 13x9" baking dish. Pour the remaining tomatoes over the zucchini. Bake for 25 minutes.

Remove from the oven and top with cheese. Bake for 5 more minutes or until the cheese is melted and bubbly. Sprinkle with fresh cilantro.

Serves 6

Black-Eyed Peas

Black-eyed peas are a favorite in San Antonio, sitting on the side of a dinner plate with beef, pork, or chicken.

3 tbsp. butter
1 small red onion, chopped
¼ cup chopped red bell pepper
1 tbsp. minced garlic
2 15.5 oz. cans black-eyed peas, drained and rinsed
1 4.5 oz. can diced green chiles, with juice
½ cup mild salsa

Melt the butter in a saucepan over medium-high heat. Add the onion, bell pepper, and garlic. Sauté until soft.

Add the black-eyed peas, chiles, and salsa. Stir to mix. Bring to a boil, then reduce the heat to low and simmer for 5 minutes.

Serves 6

Variation: To make **Bacon Black-Eyed Peas,** add 6 slices chopped bacon. Cook the bacon in a saucepan until crisp. Remove and set aside to drain on paper towels. Remove all but 2 tbsp. drippings from the saucepan. Omit the butter and continue with the recipe, sautéing the onion, bell pepper, and garlic in the bacon drippings. Return the bacon to the pan with the black-eyes peas, chiles, and salsa.

Cheese-and-Potato-Stuffed Poblanos

Stuffed with potatoes and cheese, these poblano peppers are fried until golden brown and crisp. Poblano peppers are similar to green bell peppers but have a bit more bite.

6 poblano peppers
2 medium potatoes, peeled and chopped into ½" cubes
1 8 oz. package cream cheese, softened
1¾ cups grated cheddar cheese
1 tsp. salt, divided
½ tsp. ground black pepper
2 medium eggs, separated
1 cup flour
½ tsp. white pepper
Vegetable oil for frying

Make a slit down one side of each poblano pepper. Do not cut all the way through. Place peppers in a 12" skillet over medium to medium-high heat, turning them frequently with tongs until the skin blisters.

Place them in a plastic Ziploc bag and seal the top to keep the steam in. Set aside for 20 minutes. When cool enough to handle, peel off the skins and remove the seeds through the slits, keeping the peppers whole. Dry them gently with paper towels and set aside.

While the peppers are cooling, bring a small saucepan of water to a boil. Place the potatoes in the pan. Bring to a boil again, then reduce the heat and simmer for 5 minutes. Drain.

Put the softened cream cheese in a medium-size bowl. Add cheddar cheese, ½ tsp. salt, and black pepper.

Add the potatoes and mix gently, being careful not to break up the potatoes.

Spoon the potato-cheese mixture into each pepper through the slits. Push the slits together to enclose the filling. Place the peppers on a plate, cover with plastic wrap, and refrigerate for 1 hour to allow the filling to become firm.

Add the egg whites into a small bowl and whisk them into firm peaks.

In a separate, medium-size bowl, beat the egg yolks until frothy, then fold in the whites. Scrape the mixture onto a dinner plate.

Spread the flour on another plate and season it with the remaining salt and white pepper.

Heat the vegetable oil, about 1" deep, in a deep frying pan.

Coat the poblano peppers in the flour, then in the eggs.

Fry the poblano peppers in batches until they are golden brown and crisp, turning with a spatula. Drain on paper towels and serve hot.

Serves 6

Chile Rellenos with Sauce

There are many variations of chile rellenos. They can be stuffed with a mixture of cheeses, vegetables, a meat sauce, or any combination of these and are most often served with a tomato-based sauce. They can be a little tricky to stuff, as they tend to fall apart, but are well worth the effort.

6 large poblano peppers
3 tbsp. butter
1 large onion, thinly sliced
1½ cups coarsely chopped tomatoes
½ cup chicken broth
Salt and black pepper to taste
1¾ cups grated cheddar cheese
1 large egg, separated
¼ cup flour
¼ cup vegetable oil
Sour cream

Make a slit down one side of each poblano pepper. Do not cut all the way through. Place them in a 12" skillet over medium to medium-high heat, turning them frequently with tongs until the skin blisters.

Place them in a plastic Ziploc bag and seal the top to keep the steam in. Set aside for 20 minutes. When cool enough to handle, peel off the skins and remove the seeds through the slits, keeping the peppers whole. Dry them gently with paper towels and set aside.

While the peppers are cooling, make the sauce. Melt the butter in a 10" skillet over medium-low heat. Add the onion and sauté until soft, about 7 minutes.

Add the tomatoes, broth, salt, and black pepper. Cook for 5 more minutes. Set the sauce aside and keep warm.

Mold the cheese into 6 sausage-shaped logs. Insert the cheese "logs" into each pepper. Fold the pepper tightly around the cheese filling and flatten slightly. Set aside.

In a large mixing bowl, beat the egg white until it peaks. Add the yolk and beat just to incorporate.

Put the flour on a dinner plate and roll the peppers in the flour to dust them all over.

Holding the stem of the pepper, carefully twist each poblano in the egg mixture to coat it thickly.

Heat the vegetable oil in a deep frying pan over medium-high heat. Cook the poblano peppers, 2 or 3 at a time, for about 2 minutes on each side, using tongs or a spatula to turn.

Spoon the sauce onto a dinner plate. Arrange the poblano pepper on top of the sauce and top with a dollop of sour cream.

Serves 6

Chorizo Calabacitas

Calabacitas are squash. This vegetable side dish feeds 4 to 6 people. If you have leftovers, they taste great mixed in an omelet and topped with salsa.

½ lb. chorizo sausage
1 tsp. butter
1 tsp. olive oil
1 large onion, chopped
1 garlic clove, minced
1 red bell pepper, sliced
1 green bell pepper, sliced
3 large tomatoes, chopped
4 medium yellow squash, thinly sliced
4 medium zucchini, thinly sliced
1 10 oz. package frozen corn, thawed
3 tbsp. freshly chopped cilantro
Salt and black pepper to taste
1 cup shredded Mexican Blend cheese

Cook the chorizo in a 10" skillet over medium-high heat until browned. Drain and set aside.

Melt the butter with the olive oil in a large saucepan over medium heat. Add the onion and sauté for 2 minutes, then add the garlic, bell peppers, and tomatoes. Cook for 2 more minutes.

Reduce the heat to low. Add the squash, zucchini, corn, cilantro, salt, and black pepper. Cook for 10 minutes or until the vegetables are almost done.

Add the cooked chorizo and stir to mix.

Top with cheese, then cover the pan and let cook for 2 to 3 minutes to melt the cheese.

Serves 4

Chilaquiles Calabacitas

1 tbsp. olive oil
1 medium onion, diced
1 medium zucchini, grated
1 15 oz. can black beans, drained and rinsed
1 14.5 oz. can diced tomatoes
1½ cups frozen corn, thawed
1 tsp. ground cumin
½ tsp. salt
12 corn tortillas, quartered
1 19 oz. can red or green enchilada sauce
1¼ cups shredded cheddar cheese

Preheat the oven to 400 degrees. Lightly spray a 13x9" baking dish with nonstick cooking spray. Set aside.

Heat the oil in a 12" skillet over medium-high heat. Add the onion and cook, stirring often, until it begins to brown, about 5 minutes. Stir in the zucchini, beans, tomatoes, corn, cumin, and salt. Cook, stirring occasionally, until the vegetables are heated through, about 3 minutes.

Scatter half of the tortilla pieces in the prepared baking dish. Top with half of the vegetable mixture, half of the enchilada sauce, and half of the cheese. Repeat. Cover with aluminum foil and bake for 15 minutes. Remove the aluminum foil and continue baking for 10 more minutes until the casserole is bubbling around the edges and the cheese is melted.

Serves 4

Chipotle Mushrooms

2 chipotle peppers
¼ cup butter
1 medium onion, finely chopped
2 garlic cloves, crushed
3 16 oz. containers button mushrooms
Salt and black pepper to taste
1 small bunch cilantro, coarsely chopped

Soak the dried chipotle peppers in a bowl of hot water to cover for 10 minutes or until the peppers are soft. Drain, seed, and chop.

Melt the butter in a 12" skillet over medium to medium-high heat. Add the onion, garlic, peppers, and mushrooms. Stir until they are evenly coated in the butter. Cook, stirring once or twice, until the onions and mushrooms are browned and tender, and the liquid has evaporated. Season to taste with salt and black pepper.

Place the mushrooms in a serving bowl. Garnish with cilantro.

Serves 6

Chuckwagon Corn

I found this frozen vegetable mix in the H-E-B chain of grocery stores in San Antonio the first time I came to visit. When I returned to Chicago, I couldn't find it in any grocery store; however, I did find it in cans with the name Mexicorn.

1 10 oz. bag frozen corn
1 small green bell pepper, chopped
1 small red bell pepper, chopped
1 small onion, chopped
3 to 4 tbsp. butter
Salt and black pepper to taste

Place all the ingredients in a medium-size saucepan. Cover with water. Bring to a boil, then reduce the heat, cover, and simmer for 10 to 15 minutes or until the peppers are tender.

Serves 4

Chile Corn Casserole

1 cup sour cream
1 tsp. chicken bouillon granules
½ tsp. seasoned salt
¼ tsp. dry mustard
1 4.5 oz. can diced green chiles, with juice
2 tbsp. butter, melted
1 32 oz. package frozen corn, thawed
½ cup crushed tortilla chips

Preheat the oven to 350 degrees. Lightly butter a 13x9" glass baking dish. Set aside.

In a large mixing bowl, combine the sour cream, chicken bouillon granules, seasoned salt, dry mustard, green chiles, and melted butter.

Add the corn. Combine well with the sour cream mixture.

Place the mixture in the prepared baking dish. Evenly sprinkle the crushed tortilla chips over the top. Bake for 30 minutes or until heated through.

Serves 4

Eggplant Casserole

This is San Antonio's answer to Eggplant Parmesan. The chiles and cumin give it a nice kick.

1 large eggplant
Salt to taste
⅓ cup vegetable oil
1 19 oz. can enchilada sauce
1 4.5 oz. can diced green chiles, with juice
½ cup thinly sliced green onions
½ tsp. ground cumin
½ tsp. garlic salt
¼ cup sliced black olives
1½ cups grated cheddar cheese, divided
1 8 oz. container sour cream

Cut the unpeeled eggplant into ½" slices, crosswise. Season them lightly with salt and place them in a colander to drain for 20 minutes.

Preheat the oven to 450 degrees. Lightly spray a 13x9" baking dish with cooking spray. Set aside.

Place the drained eggplant slices on a large baking sheet. Brush both sides with the vegetable oil. Bake for 15 to 20 minutes or until they are lightly browned and crisp. Remove the eggplant slices and reduce the oven temperature to 350 degrees.

While the eggplant slices are baking, combine the enchilada sauce, chiles, onions, cumin, garlic salt, and olives in a medium-size saucepan. Simmer for 10 minutes.

Line the prepared baking dish with half of the cooked eggplant slices. Spoon half of the enchilada sauce mixture over. Sprinkle with half of the cheese. Repeat.

Bake for 25 minutes or until bubbly and the cheese is lightly brown.

Serve with sour cream on the side.

Serves 6

Stewed Okra

3 to 4 tbsp. butter
1 cup fresh or frozen okra, cut into ½" slices
¼ cup chopped green bell pepper
½ cup chopped onion
1 tbsp. cayenne pepper
1 14.5 oz. can diced tomatoes, with juice
Salt to taste

Melt the butter in a 12" skillet over medium-low heat. Add the okra, bell pepper, onion, and cayenne pepper. Sauté until the vegetables are tender.

Add the tomatoes and salt to taste. Heat through.

Serves 4

Peasant Potatoes

These potatoes add spicy heat to your meal. Leftovers are great for breakfast, accompanying eggs and chorizo.

4 tbsp. vegetable oil, divided
1 medium onion, finely chopped
1 lb. yellow potatoes, scrubbed and cut into ½" cubes
6 jalapeño peppers, roasted, seeded, and chopped
1 cup grated cheddar cheese
Freshly chopped cilantro

Heat half of the oil in a 12" skillet over medium heat. Add the onion and sauté for 3 to 4 minutes or until soft.

Add the potato cubes. Stir to coat them with the oil, then cover the pan and cook for 20 to 25 minutes or until the potatoes are tender, shaking the pan occasionally to prevent them from sticking to the bottom.

Push the potatoes to the side of the skillet, then add the remaining oil.

When the oil is hot, spread out the potatoes and add the jalapeños. Cook over high heat for 5 to 10 minutes, stirring carefully so that the potatoes turn golden brown all over but do not break up.

Sprinkle with cheese and cilantro. Cover the pan until the cheese melts.

Serves 4

Pimiento Potatoes

Butter for the baking dish
⅓ cup butter
3 tbsp. flour
2 cups milk
2 cups shredded Monterey jack cheese, divided
1 2 oz. jar diced pimientos, drained
1 4.5 oz. can chopped green chiles, drained
½ tsp. salt
2 lb. baking potatoes, peeled and thinly sliced, about 3 cups

Preheat the oven to 350 degrees. Lightly butter a 13x9" baking dish. Set aside.

Melt ⅓ cup butter in a medium saucepan over low heat. Add the flour, stirring until smooth, then add the milk. Cook, stirring constantly, until the mixture is slightly thickened.

Stir in 1½ cups of the cheese. Remove the pan from the heat and stir until the cheese melts.

Add the pimientos, green chiles, and salt, stirring well.

Place half of the potato slices in the prepared baking dish. Top with half of the cheese mixture. Repeat layers.

Bake, covered, for 20 minutes, then uncover and bake for 40 more minutes.

Sprinkle with the remaining ½ cup of cheese and bake for 5 more minutes.

Serves 6

Poblano Cheese Potatoes

3 lb. red potatoes, scrubbed
1 tbsp. olive oil
5 poblano peppers, stemmed, seeded, and diced
1 medium onion, chopped
2 cups whipping cream
1 cup milk
2 garlic cloves
Salt and black pepper to taste
2½ cups grated sharp cheddar cheese

Cook the potatoes in a pot of salted boiling water until tender, about 25 minutes. Drain the potatoes in a colander and let cool completely.

When cool, peel and slice the potatoes into ½" thick rounds. Place in a large mixing bowl.

Heat the oil in a 12" skillet over medium-high heat. Add the poblano peppers and onion. Sauté until the onion is very soft, about 15 minutes. Transfer the mixture to a food processor.

Add the cream, milk, and garlic. Blend to form a thick sauce.

Season the sauce to taste with salt and pepper. Pour the sauce over the potatoes. Stir gently to coat.

Preheat the oven to 350 degrees. Lightly spray a 13x9" baking dish with nonstick cooking spray.

Overlap half of the potatoes with the sauce in the bottom of the prepared baking dish. Sprinkle with half the cheese. Add the remaining potatoes and sauce, then top with the remaining cheese. Bake until heated through and brown on top, about 30 minutes.

Serves 6

Poblano Potatoes

These potatoes pack a powerful punch.

2 lb. red potatoes, scrubbed and chopped
1½ tbsp. salt
1 cup sour cream
½ cup milk
5 poblano peppers, roasted, peeled, seeded, and diced
Salt and black pepper to taste

Place the potatoes in a large saucepan with enough water to cover. Add the salt and bring to a boil, then reduce the heat and simmer, uncovered, until soft, about 20 minutes.

Drain, then return the potatoes to the pan. Mash with a potato masher until the potatoes are slightly chunky.

Add the sour cream, milk, and poblano peppers. Stir to mix. Season with salt and black pepper to taste.

Serves 6

Poncho Baked Potato

4 large baking potatoes, scrubbed
1½ lb. lean ground beef
1 small onion, finely chopped
1 10¼ oz. can beef gravy
1 15.5 oz. can red kidney beans, drained
2 tbsp. chili powder
2 tbsp. ketchup
1 garlic clove, minced
1 jalapeño pepper, finely chopped
Butter for the baked potatoes
Black pepper to taste
Paprika to taste
1 cup shredded cheddar cheese
1 cup shredded Monterey jack cheese

Preheat the oven to 350 degrees. Prick each potato several times with the tines of a fork. Place in the oven and cook for 1 hour, 15 minutes.

During the last 30 minutes of baking time, cook the ground beef and onion over medium-high heat in a 12" skillet until the beef is browned and the onion is tender.

Add the gravy, beans, chili powder, ketchup, garlic, and jalapeño. Heat to boiling, then reduce the heat and simmer for 20 minutes, stirring occasionally.

Remove the potatoes from the oven and split them lengthwise. Butter them and sprinkle with black pepper and paprika.

Spoon the gravy mixture generously over the baked potatoes. Sprinkle with the cheeses.

Serves 4

San Antonio Skins

4 large baking potatoes, scrubbed
1 to 2 tbsp. vegetable oil
Salt and black pepper to taste
1 cup Mexican Velveeta cheese
1 tsp. Tabasco® sauce
10 strips bacon, crisp-cooked and crumbled
4 green onions, chopped, divided
1 cup shredded cheddar cheese
1 8 oz. container sour cream

Preheat the oven to 350 degrees. Prick each potato several times with the tines of a fork. Rub each potato with vegetable oil. Place the potatoes in the oven and cook for 1 hour, 15 minutes. Remove the potatoes and turn the oven to broil.

Split the baked potatoes lengthwise. Scoop out the pulp, reserving it for another use. Sprinkle each potato skin with salt and black pepper.

Melt the Velveeta cheese in a small saucepan over low heat. Stir in the Tabasco® sauce.

Place equal amounts of the cheese mixture in each potato skin. Top with equal amounts of bacon and ¾ of the green onions. Top with the cheddar cheese.

Broil the potato skins until the cheddar cheese is bubbling. Garnish with the remaining green onions and sour cream.

Serves 8

Variation: To make **Broccoli Skins,** top the cheese sauce in the potato with 1½ cups cooked, chopped broccoli and continue with the recipe. To make **Chicken Chile Skins,** top the cheese sauce in the potato with 1 cup minced, cooked chicken and ¼ cup diced green chiles and continue with the recipe.

Black Bean Tortilla Lasagna

This lasagna, southwest style, offers a vegetarian take on the classic version. Add ½ lb. each cooked lean ground beef and chorizo sausage to make a meaty meal.

1 15 oz. container ricotta cheese
⅓ cup grated cheddar cheese
1 medium egg
¼ cup milk
4 tbsp. freshly chopped cilantro, divided
1 28 oz. can enchilada sauce
9 8" flour tortillas
2 15 oz. cans black beans, drained and rinsed
1 4 oz. can diced green chiles, drained
1½ cups fresh chopped spinach
2 cups shredded Monterey jack cheese

Preheat the oven to 350 degrees.

In a medium-size bowl, mix the ricotta and cheddar cheeses together with the egg, milk, and half the cilantro.

Spread a thin layer of enchilada sauce in a 13x9" glass baking dish. Layer 3 tortillas, cutting them if necessary, with one-third each of the beans, chiles, spinach, ricotta mixture, and Monterey jack cheese. Cover with enchilada sauce. Repeat twice to make three layers.

Sprinkle the top with the remaining cilantro. Cover tightly with aluminum foil and bake for 30 minutes. Remove the foil and bake for 10 more minutes to brown the cheese.

Serves 6

Black Bean Patties

2 15 oz. cans black beans, drained and rinsed
6 green onions, finely chopped
1 red bell pepper, finely chopped
¼ cup chopped fresh cilantro
2 garlic cloves, minced
1½ tbsp. minced seeded jalapeño pepper
2 tsp. ground cumin
Salt and black pepper to taste
1 large egg
2 tbsp. plus 1 cup yellow cornmeal
6 tbsp. olive oil, divided
Sour cream
Salsa

Place the beans in a large bowl. Using a potato masher, coarsely mash the beans.

Mix in the green onions, red bell pepper, cilantro, garlic, jalapeño, and cumin. Season to taste with salt and black pepper.

Mix in the egg and 2 tbsp. cornmeal.

Place the remaining 1 cup cornmeal in a small dish. Drop 1 heaping spoonful of the bean mixture into the cornmeal. Turn to coat. Flatten into a ½" thick patty. Repeat, making 18 patties.

Heat 3 tbsp. of the oil in a 12" skillet over medium heat. Working in batches, fry the bean patties until firm and crisp, about 6 minutes per side. Add more oil as needed. Drain the patties on paper towels.

Serve warm with sour cream and salsa.

Serves 6

Basic Black Beans

It doesn't get much easier than this.

1 15 oz. can black beans, drained and rinsed
1 tbsp. water
¼ tsp. onion powder
¼ tsp. chili powder
⅛ tsp. paprika
⅛ tsp. garlic powder
Salt and black pepper to taste

Mix all the ingredients together in a small bowl. Cover loosely with plastic wrap and microwave on high for 1 minute. Stir and serve.

Serves 4

Broiled Salsa Beans

1 16 oz. can refried beans
1 15.5 oz. can pinto beans, drained and rinsed
½ cup salsa
⅔ cup grated sharp cheddar cheese, divided
2 green onions, sliced

Preheat the broiler. Position the rack in the upper third of the oven.

Combine the refried beans, pinto beans, salsa, and ⅓ cup of the cheese in a medium saucepan. Cook over medium heat, stirring, until the mixture is hot and the cheese is melted, 6 to 8 minutes.

Spoon the bean mixture into a 2-qt. baking dish and sprinkle with the remaining ⅓ cup cheese and green onions. Broil until the cheese is lightly browned, about 2 minutes.

Serves 4

Beer Beans

This recipe involves a lot of prep time, but the beans practically cook by themselves with just a little help from you.

1 ham hock
5½ cups water
1 medium onion, finely diced, divided
1¼ cups dry pinto beans, soaked overnight and drained
1 tbsp. vegetable oil
2 jalapeño peppers, peeled, seeded, and diced
1 tbsp. cumin seed
1 tbsp. chili powder
1 12 oz. can beer
1 14.5 oz. can diced tomatoes
2 tbsp. freshly chopped cilantro
Salt to taste

Simmer the ham hock in water in a large saucepan for 1½ hours. Skim the fat, or refrigerate until the fat can be scraped off. Reserve the stock.

Combine the ham hock, ham stock, half of the onion, and the pinto beans in a 6-qt. stockpot. Bring to a boil, then reduce the heat and simmer for 2 hours or until the beans are tender. Add more boiling water if necessary.

Heat the oil in a 12" skillet over medium-high heat. Add the remaining onion, jalapeño peppers, cumin, and chili powder. Sauté for 5 minutes or until the onion browns.

Add the beer, tomatoes, and cilantro. Cook for 2 more minutes.

Add the beer mixture to the bean mixture. Season with salt to taste.

Serves 6

Charro Beans

Charro beans are whole not mashed beans.

2 15.5 oz. cans pinto beans, drained and rinsed
½ cup Mexican beer
6 jalapeño peppers, roasted, seeded, and chopped
2 medium tomatoes, peeled and chopped
1 tsp. ground cinnamon
3 tbsp. butter
1 medium onion, chopped
2 garlic cloves, crushed

Place the pinto beans and beer in a large saucepan. Turn the heat to high. Cook for 5 minutes or until some of the beer has been absorbed.

Reduce the heat to medium. Stir in the jalapeños, then add the tomatoes and cinnamon. Cook for 10 more minutes, stirring occasionally.

While this is cooking, melt the butter in a 10" skillet over medium heat. Add the onion and garlic. Cook for 4 to 5 minutes or until the onion is soft.

Add the onion-garlic mixture to the beans. Stir to mix.

Serves 4

Cowboy Beans

5 cups water
1 lb. dried pinto beans, picked over and rinsed
1 12 oz. bottle dark beer
1 medium onion, chopped
4 bacon slices, cut into ½" pieces
4 garlic cloves, finely chopped
1 tsp. minced canned chipotle chiles
Salt and black pepper to taste

Place 5 cups water in a heavy stockpot. Add the pinto beans, beer, onion, bacon, garlic, and chipotle chiles. Gently simmer, uncovered, over medium-low heat for 2½ hours or until the beans are tender and the liquid is reduced enough to cover beans by 1", adding more water if necessary and stirring occasionally. Season to taste with salt and black pepper.

Serves 6

Drunken Beans

The beans aren't really drunk; they're just cooked in beer. They are also referred to as frijoles borracho. The beans are whole and served in their broth.

- 2 cups dried pinto beans, picked over and rinsed
- ½ lb. bacon, chopped
- 1 large white onion, chopped
- 1 tbsp. dried oregano
- 1 garlic clove, finely chopped
- 1½ qt. water
- ½ cup sliced pickled jalapeño peppers
- 1 12 oz. bottle dark beer, such as Dos Equis
- 2 tsp. salt, or more to taste

Soak the beans in a large bowl of cold water for 4 to 6 hours. Drain.

Preheat the oven to 300 degrees.

In a large heavy ovenproof pan, cook the bacon, onion, oregano, and garlic over medium-high heat, stirring, until the onion is lightly browned. Drain.

Add the beans, water, jalapeños, and beer. Bring to a boil and let boil for 1 minute.

Place the pan in the middle of the oven and bake for 1½ to 2 hours or until the beans are soft. Add additional water if the beans begin to dry out. The mixture will be soupy.

Remove from the oven and add 2 tsp. salt. Bake the beans for 10 more minutes. Taste, and add more salt if necessary.

Serves 6

Peppered Pinto Beans

Season beans with salt to taste when they are done cooking. Adding salt during cooking toughens the beans.

5 strips bacon, chopped
1 small onion, diced
8 cups water
2 cups dried pinto beans, picked over and rinsed
½ tsp. red pepper flakes
1 tsp. onion powder
1 tsp. garlic powder
¼ tsp. black pepper
¼ tsp. rubbed sage
¼ tsp. ground cumin
¼ tsp. chili powder
2 chicken bouillon cubes
Salt to taste

Cook the bacon with the onion in a large, heavy stockpot over medium-high heat. Drain.

Add all the remaining ingredients, except the salt. Bring to a boil and let boil for 15 minutes. Reduce the heat to low, cover, and simmer for 4 hours, stirring occasionally and adding more water if necessary.

With a potato masher, mash about half of the beans while still in the pot. This will help to thicken the sauce. Cook for 30 more minutes. Season to taste with salt.

Serves 6

Perfect Pintos

These are traditionally cooked in a clay pot, which adds a wonderful earthy flavor, but a heavy stock pot will do.

1½ cups dried pinto beans, soaked overnight in water to cover
2½ cups water
2 medium onions, coarsely chopped
10 garlic cloves, coarsely chopped
10 strips bacon, coarsely chopped
1 small bunch cilantro, divided
Salt and black pepper to taste

Drain the beans in a colander, rinse them under cold running water, and drain again.

Pour 2½ cups water in a large, heavy stockpot. Bring to a boil, then add the beans.

Bring to a boil again. Add the onions, garlic cloves, and bacon. Bring to a boil again, then reduce the heat and simmer for 1½ hours or until the beans are tender and there is only a little liquid remaining.

Ladle about 1 cup of the beans and a little bit of liquid into a blender. Process until smooth.

Return the blended beans to the saucepan. Stir.

Add most of the cilantro. Season with salt and black pepper. Stir to mix well.

Ladle the beans into individual serving bowls. Sprinkle with the remaining cilantro.

Serves 6

Quickie Pintos

This easy recipe starts with a can of pinto beans. The additional ingredients add spicy heat.

2 tsp. olive oil
1 small onion, chopped
1 garlic clove, minced
½ jalapeño pepper, minced
½ tsp. chili powder
1 15.5 oz. can pinto beans, drained and rinsed
2 tbsp. water
¼ tsp. cumin
¼ tsp. salt
1 tbsp. chopped fresh cilantro

Heat the oil in a medium-size saucepan over medium-high heat. Add the onion, garlic, jalapeño, and chili powder. Sauté until the vegetables are softened.

Add the beans, water, cumin, and salt. Coarsely mash about half the beans in the pan. Reduce the heat and simmer until heated through. Stir in the cilantro.

Serves 4

Red Rice

My daughter, Jennifer, makes the best rice. Every time we get together for a Mexican meal, we always beg her to make this dish. Rice is the accompaniment to numerous meals, and there are many recipes for rice. One of the secrets of great rice is to toast it first, which adds an entirely new dimension to the flavor.

1 14.5 oz. can chicken broth
¼ tsp. cumin
¼ tsp. garlic salt
1 packet Sazón Goya con culantro y achiote* (coriander and annatto)
3 tbsp. tomato sauce
2 to 3 tbsp. butter
1 cup rice

Mix together the chicken broth, cumin, garlic salt, Sazón Goya seasoning, and tomato sauce in a small bowl.

Melt the butter in a medium-size saucepan over medium heat. Add the rice and brown it.

Add the broth mixture. Bring to a boil, then reduce the heat, cover and simmer for 15 to 20 minutes or until all the liquid is absorbed.

Serves 4

***Note:** The Sazón Goya seasoning is sold in the grocery store in the ethnic section, next to the rice and beans. It comes in a 1.41-oz. box with 8 seasoning packets.

Poblano Rice

2 poblano peppers, roasted, seeded, and chopped
1 small green bell pepper, roasted, seeded, and chopped
1 garlic clove, coarsely chopped
1 large bunch cilantro, coarsely chopped
2 cups chicken broth
2 tbsp. vegetable oil
1 small onion, finely chopped
1 cup long-grain white rice
Salt and black pepper to taste

Put the poblano peppers, bell pepper, garlic, and cilantro into a blender.

Add the chicken broth and blend until smooth.

Heat the oil in a 12" skillet over medium heat. Add the onion and rice. Cook for 5 minutes or until the rice is golden and the onion is translucent.

Stir in the poblano mixture. Bring to a boil, then reduce the heat, cover, and cook for 25 to 30 minutes or until all the liquid is absorbed. Season with salt and black pepper to taste.

Serves 4

Red Rice and Beans

Rice and beans are served with almost everything in San Antonio. Sometimes they're mixed together, as in this recipe; other times they're served side-by-side with whatever you're eating or on a combination plate with chopped lettuce, tomatoes, and guacamole on the side.

1 cup tomato juice
½ tsp. garlic powder
⅛ tsp. cayenne pepper
¼ tsp. cumin
1 15.5 oz. can dark red kidney beans, rinsed, drained, and slightly mashed
3 cups hot, cooked white rice
1 cup shredded cheddar cheese

In a medium-size saucepan, heat the tomato juice, garlic powder, cayenne pepper, cumin, and beans to boiling. Stir to mix.

Reduce the heat to low. Cover and cook for 5 minutes, stirring occasionally.

Stir in the cooked rice and heat through. Place on individual plates (with your main dish) and sprinkle with cheddar cheese.

Serves 4

Optional Add-ins: Sauté ½ cup each onion and green bell pepper in 2 tbsp. butter, then follow the above recipe.

Sandwiches, Quesadillas, and Tacos

Chili Burgers

1½ lb. lean ground beef
1 medium tomato, chopped
½ cup black olives, chopped
1 tsp. finely minced garlic
½ tsp. Dijon mustard
1 tbsp. chili powder
¼ tsp. dried basil
¼ tsp. dried oregano
Grated zest of 1 lemon
2 tbsp. chopped fresh parsley
Salt and black pepper to taste
4 hamburger buns, lightly toasted on a grill or under the broiler
⅓ cup sour cream
3 green onions, chopped
½ cup grated Monterey jack cheese

In a large mixing bowl, combine the ground beef, tomato, olives, garlic, mustard, chili powder, basil, oregano, lemon zest, parsley, salt, and black pepper. Shape into 4 patties. Grill or broil the patties.

Serve on buns. Top with sour cream, green onions, and cheese.

Serves 4

Black Bean Burgers

These black bean burgers, served at EZ's Brick Oven & Grill, are the best burgers I've ever had. The first time I visited San Antonio, my daughter took me to lunch there, and we ate there several more times before I had to fly home to cold Chicago. Now I live in San Antonio and can eat at EZ's, sitting outside in the warm, sunny weather, any time I want to.

1 lb. lean ground beef
½ 15 oz. can black beans, drained, rinsed, and slightly mashed
½ cup Fritos®, slightly crushed
Warm hamburger buns or Texas rolls
¼ cup picante sauce, warmed
½ cup shredded cheddar cheese
½ cup guacamole

Shape the ground beef into patties. Grill or broil until done.

While this is cooking, heat the black beans in a small saucepan or in the microwave.

Assemble the sandwich with a layer of Fritos® on the bottom of the bun, spread the picante sauce over, place the patty on top of this, spread the mashed black beans over the patty, sprinkle with cheese, spread on the guacamole, place the top of the bun on, and enjoy.

Serves 4

Tex-Mex Turkey Burgers

- 1 8 oz. package sliced mushrooms, finely chopped
- ¾ cup chopped zucchini
- ½ cup finely chopped onion
- ½ cup finely chopped red bell pepper
- 1¼ lb. lean ground turkey
- 1½ tbsp. taco seasoning mix
- ¾ cup shredded cheddar cheese
- 6 hamburger buns
- ¼ cup plus 2 tbsp. salsa
- 6 leaves romaine lettuce, chopped

Place the mushrooms, zucchini, onion, red bell pepper, turkey, and taco seasoning mix in a medium-size bowl. Mix thoroughly. Shape into 6 patties.

Grill the patties over medium coals or cook under a broiler for about 6 minutes on each side or until the patties are cooked through. Alternatively, coat a 12" nonstick skillet with cooking spray and cook the patties over medium heat for about 5 minutes per side. To retain the moisture, do not flatten or press down on the patties while they are cooking.

Sprinkle equal amounts of cheese over each patty and cook for 1 more minute, just until the cheese is melted.

Place each patty on a bun and top with salsa and lettuce.

Serves 6

Broiled Bean Sandwich

Good for either breakfast or lunch.

2 soft sub rolls
1½ tbsp. butter
¾ cup refried beans, heated
1½ cups shredded Mexican Blend cheese
½ cup salsa, heated

Preheat the broiler.

Split the rolls lengthwise and spread with butter. Place on a baking sheet and broil until lightly toasted to a golden brown.

Spread each half with refried beans, then sprinkle with cheese. Return to the broiler for about 3 minutes or until the cheese is bubbly.

Spoon the salsa over and serve hot.

Serves 2

Chicken Black Bean Torta

Tortas are traditionally made with bolillos, a plain, crisp, white roll that has the doughy filling pulled out before adding the sandwich ingredients. If you are unable to find bolillos, use small, crisp French rolls. Pull out the bready dough inside and stuff the rolls with this recipe.

2 tbsp. butter
4 bolillos, or French bread rolls, cut in half lengthwise, excess dough removed from both halves
1 cup refried black beans
8 tbsp. grated Mexican Blend cheese
1 chicken breast, cut crosswise into 4 thin slices and pounded to ⅛" thickness
Salt and black pepper to taste
Olive oil cooking spray
4 green onions, coarsely chopped

Preheat the broiler. Lightly butter the outside of the bolillos. Toast under the broiler until golden, about 3 minutes.

Spread the inside with black beans, sprinkle with cheese, and cover with aluminum foil to keep warm.

Season the chicken with salt and black pepper.

Spray a 10" skillet with cooking spray. Heat over high heat. Add the chicken and sauté for about 1 minute on each side or until cooked through.

Place the chicken on top of the bean and cheese mixture. Top with the green onions and toast under the broiler for 1 more minute. Put the bolillos halves together and enjoy.

Serves 2

Pork Torta

The essential ingredients in a torta are refried beans and chile peppers. After that, it's up to your imagination and your taste buds. You can substitute chicken, turkey, or ham for pork.

2 jalapeño peppers, seeded and cut into thin strips
Juice of ½ lime
⅔ cup refried beans
4 bolillos, or French bread rolls, cut in half lengthwise, excess dough removed from both halves
2 slices cooked roast pork, cut into thin strips
1 tomato, sliced
4 slices cheddar cheese
4 tbsp. cilantro, chopped
4 tbsp. sour cream
1 cup shredded lettuce, tossed lightly with olive oil

Preheat the oven to 350 degrees.

Add the jalapeño peppers to a small bowl. Squeeze the lime juice over them. Set aside.

Spread the refried beans onto the bottom half of the bread. Place the sliced pork on top of the beans. Top with the sliced tomato.

Drain the jalapeño strips, then put them on top of the tomato slices. Add the cheese and sprinkle with cilantro.

Wrap each sandwich in aluminum foil. Place in the oven for 5 to 10 minutes or until heated through. Remove from the oven and open the sandwiches. Add the sour cream and lettuce. Put the torta back together and enjoy.

Serves 4

Cheddar Chicken Burritos

2 to 3 tbsp. olive oil
2 skinless, boneless chicken breasts, cut into bite-size pieces
½ red bell pepper, chopped
2 tbsp. chopped onion
1 tsp. chopped garlic
½ tsp. dried cilantro
½ tsp. dried basil
¼ tsp. cumin
1 small tomato, diced
¼ cup grated cheddar cheese
5 7" flour tortillas

Preheat the oven to 350 degrees. Lightly spray an 8x8" baking dish with nonstick cooking spray. Set aside.

Heat the oil in a 10" skillet over medium-high heat.

Add the chicken, bell pepper, onion, garlic, cilantro, basil, and cumin. Cook for 10 minutes, stirring occasionally, or until the chicken is done and the vegetables are soft.

Add the tomato and cheese. Heat through.

Soften the tortillas by placing them, stacked together, in the microwave for 15 seconds. This will prevent them from tearing and make it easier to roll them.

Spoon the filling onto each tortilla. Roll tightly and place them seam side down in the prepared baking dish. Bake for 15 minutes or until heated through.

Serves 4

Variation: For **Pork Burritos,** substitute ½ lb. pork tenderloin for the chicken and use green bell pepper instead of red bell pepper.

Chicken and Bean Burritos

2 to 3 tbsp. olive oil
2 skinless, boneless chicken breasts, cut into small bite-size pieces
1 tsp. cumin
1 tsp. garlic powder
1 15 oz. can black beans, drained and rinsed, or substitute kidney beans or pinto beans
1 cup fresh or frozen corn, thawed
½ cup thick and chunky salsa
1 green bell pepper, diced
8 6" white corn tortillas
½ cup grated cheddar cheese
Sour cream

Heat the oil in a 12" skillet over medium-high heat. Add the chicken and brown on all sides.

Add the cumin, garlic powder, black beans, corn, salsa, and green bell pepper. Cook for 10 minutes, stirring occasionally, or until the chicken is done and the vegetables are soft.

Soften the tortillas by placing them, stacked together, in the microwave for 15 seconds. This will prevent them from tearing and make it easier to roll them.

Spoon equal amounts of the filling onto each tortilla. Top with cheddar cheese. Fold the ends in and roll up. Serve with sour cream.

Serves 4

Chicken Quesadillas

Cheese quesadillas are often served as an appetizer with ranchero sauce or salsa for dipping. Add some extra fillings and these tortilla sandwiches make a light lunch. Making a quesadilla is like making a grilled cheese sandwich, San Antonio style.

6 8" flour tortillas
1½ cups shredded Mexican Blend cheese
1 4.5 oz. can diced green chiles, drained
1 cup cooked chicken, shredded
1 small tomato, seeded and chopped
3 tbsp. finely chopped green onions
1 tbsp. chopped cilantro
Salsa
Sour cream

Heat a 10" nonstick skillet over medium heat. Lay 1 tortilla in the skillet. Cook for 1 to 2 minutes or until the tortilla is lightly browned on the bottom. It should be soft and pliable, not crispy.

Flip the tortilla over and sprinkle ¼ of the cheese, green chiles, chicken, tomato, green onions, and cilantro over the tortilla. Cook for 1 to 2 minutes.

Fold the tortilla in half, using a spatula, trying not to spill the fillings out. Press down gently with the spatula. Remove from the skillet and keep warm. Repeat with the remaining tortillas.

Cut each quesadilla into thirds. Serve with salsa and sour cream on the side.

Serves 4

Chicken Cheddar Quesadillas

Salsa verde is made with tomatillos, which look like green tomatoes wrapped in a paperlike husk; chile peppers; and onions. To make your own, see the recipe for Tomatillo Sauce on page 223.

1½ cups medium-hot chunky salsa verde
1 cup frozen corn, thawed
1 cup red onion, divided
¼ cup chopped fresh cilantro, divided
Salt and black pepper to taste
1 lb. chicken tenders
2 tsp. chili powder
1 tsp. ground cumin
2 tbsp. olive oil
2 garlic cloves, chopped
3 11" flour tortillas
1 16 oz. package shredded cheddar cheese

Mix the salsa, corn, ¼ cup red onion, and half of the cilantro in a small bowl. Season to taste with salt and pepper.

Sprinkle chicken with chili powder and cumin.

Heat the oil in a 12" skillet over medium-high heat. Add the chicken and sauté until the chicken is almost cooked through. Add the garlic and remaining ¾ cup onion. Sauté until lightly browned. Remove the pan from the heat.

Place a tortilla in a separate 12" skillet over medium-high heat. Cook until lightly browned on the bottom. Flip the tortilla over and top with ½ cup cheese. Place one-third of the chicken mixture on top. Sprinkle with 2 tbsp. cilantro and another ½ cup cheese. When the cheese begins to melt, fold the tortilla over and remove to a plate. Repeat with the remaining tortillas.

Cut the quesadilla in wedges and serve with salsa for dipping.

Serves 4

Chipotle Chicken Quesadillas

Chipotle peppers are smoked, dried jalapeño peppers. The flavor speaks for itself.

2 skinless, boneless chicken breasts
3 canned chipotle peppers, seeded and thinly sliced
¼ cup chopped cilantro
3 green onions, trimmed and thinly sliced at an angle
6 8" flour tortillas
4 tbsp. butter, melted
2 cups shredded Mexican Blend cheese

Poach the chicken in 2 cups simmering water for 10 to 15 minutes or until the chicken is cooked through. Remove to a plate and let cool slightly, then shred with two forks.

Preheat the oven to 350 degrees.

In a large bowl, combine the chicken, chipotle peppers, cilantro, and green onions.

Brush one side of each tortilla with half of the butter. Place the tortillas, buttered side down, on a baking sheet. Brush the tops with the remaining butter.

Spread equal amounts of the cheese over each tortilla. Bake for 5 minutes or until the cheese is melted.

Spoon equal amounts of the chicken mixture over half of the tortilla, fold over to enclose, and return the tortillas to the oven for 5 minutes or until heated through. Cut into wedges and serve.

Serves 4

Grilled Chicken Quesadillas

4 skinless, boneless chicken breasts
4 tbsp. olive oil, divided
1 1.25 oz. package taco seasoning, divided
1 red bell pepper, cut into strips
1 yellow bell pepper, cut into strips
1 red onion, thinly sliced
1 tsp. minced garlic
2 tbsp. capers, drained
1 8 oz. package cream cheese, softened
1½ cups shredded Mexican Blend cheese
12 6" flour tortillas
1 tbsp. chopped cilantro
Salsa
Sour cream

Brush the chicken breasts with 2 tbsp. olive oil and sprinkle with some of the taco seasoning. Grill until done. Set aside. When cool, cut into strips.

Preheat the oven to 400 degrees.

Heat the remaining oil in a 12" skillet over medium heat. Add the red and yellow bell peppers and the onion. Sauté until tender.

Add the garlic and capers. Stir to mix. Remove the pan from the heat and set aside.

In a medium-size bowl, stir together the cream cheese, Mexican Blend cheese, and 1 tbsp. of the taco seasoning. Set aside.

Place 6 tortillas on a large baking sheet. Spread the cream cheese mixture on each tortilla. Top with the chicken strips and bell pepper mixture.

Sprinkle on the remaining taco seasoning and cilantro, then top with the remaining tortillas. Cover with aluminum foil and bake for 10 to 15 minutes or until heated through. Serve with salsa and sour cream.

Serves 6

Quickie Quesadillas

These quickie quesadillas take 10 to 15 minutes from beginning to end. Layered with flavor, they are baked rather than cooked in a skillet.

8 8" flour tortillas
Vegetable cooking spray
2 cups cooked chicken, shredded*
¾ cup taco sauce
1 16 oz. can refried beans
1 cup chopped avocado
½ cup shredded Monterey jack cheese
½ cup shredded cheddar cheese
2 green onions, sliced
Sour cream

Preheat the oven to 400 degrees.

Spray both sides of the tortillas with the cooking spray. Place the tortillas on two baking sheets. Bake until the tortillas are lightly toasted, about 3 minutes.

In a medium-size bowl, mix the cooked, shredded chicken with taco sauce.

Remove the tortillas from the oven and spread the refried beans on 4 tortillas. Top with the chicken mixture.

Sprinkle the avocado, Monterey jack and cheddar cheeses, and green onions over the chicken mixture. Top with the remaining 4 tortillas.

Return to the oven and bake for 5 minutes or until heated through and the cheese melts.

Serve with sour cream.

Serves 4

*You can buy cooked shredded chicken at the grocery store in the refrigerated section or buy a 16 oz. can cooked chicken. Drain and shred.

Terrific Tacos

There are infinite variations on tacos. They can be made with soft flour tortillas, corn tortillas, or taco shells. The main ingredients are seasoned hamburger, pork, chicken, or chorizo sausage and shredded cheese, lettuce, and tomatoes. You can add a multitude of other ingredients, such as refried beans; white, yellow, or green onions; red or green bell peppers; any chile pepper your mouth can handle; olives; corn; salsa; guacamole; and sour cream.

1 lb. ground chorizo
½ cup chopped onion
2 garlic cloves, minced
1 tbsp. chili powder
½ cup salsa
8 taco shells, warmed
1 cup shredded cheddar cheese
1 8 oz. container sour cream
1 cup chopped lettuce
1 tomato, chopped
1 avocado, diced

Cook the chorizo, onion, garlic, and chili powder in a 12" skillet over medium heat until the meat is well browned. Drain.

Add the salsa. Bring to a boil, stirring constantly.

Spoon equal amounts of the chorizo mixture into each warmed taco shell. Top with cheese, sour cream, lettuce, tomato, and avocado.

Serves 4

Soft Beef Tacos

1¼ lb. rump steak, cut into 2" cubes
2 ancho chiles, seeded
2 pasilla chiles, seeded
2 tbsp. vegetable oil
2 garlic cloves, crushed
2 tsp. dried oregano
¼ tsp. ground cumin
8 8" flour tortillas, warmed
Shredded lettuce
Chopped tomatoes

Add the meat to a saucepan and cover with water. Bring to a boil, then reduce the heat and simmer for 1 to 1½ hours.

While this is cooking, put both chiles into a small bowl. Cover with hot water and let soak for 30 minutes.

Put the chiles, with their soaking liquid, into a blender and process into a smooth paste.

Drain the meat, reserving 1 cup of the cooking liquid. Set aside.

Heat the oil in a 10" skillet over medium-high heat. Add the garlic, oregano, and cumin. Cook for 2 minutes.

Stir in the chile paste and the reserved cooking liquid from the beef. Tear 1 of the tortillas into small pieces and add it to the mixture. Bring to a boil, then reduce the heat and simmer for 10 minutes, stirring occasionally, until the sauce has thickened.

Shred the meat, using two forks, and stir it into the sauce. Simmer for 5 more minutes.

Spoon the mixture into the soft, warmed tortillas. Add the lettuce and tomatoes, then fold the tortillas over to enclose the filling.

Serves 4

Variation: To make **Sour Cream Beef Enchiladas,** use corn tortillas instead of flour tortillas. Roll up the meat mixture in the tortillas. Place in a lightly buttered 13x9" baking dish. Spread 1¼ cups sour cream and ¾ cup grated cheddar cheese over the top. Sprinkle with chopped cilantro. Place under a preheated broiler for 5 minutes or until the cheese melts and the sauce begins to bubble.

Corn and Beef Tacos

The basic ingredients in this recipe combine to make a flavorful taco.

1 lb. lean ground beef
1 15 oz. can corn, drained
1 8 oz. can tomato sauce
¾ cup water
Salt to taste
½ tsp. garlic powder
1 tsp. cumin
Warmed corn tortillas

Heat a 12" skillet over medium-high heat. Add the ground beef and cook until browned. Drain.

Add the corn, tomato sauce, and water. Stir to mix.

Add the salt, garlic powder, and cumin. Bring to a boil, then reduce the heat and simmer for 15 minutes or until the sauce has thickened.

Just before serving, warm the corn tortillas in the microwave.

Spoon the mixture into the tortillas and serve.

Serves 4

Steak and Corn Tacos, Family Style

A tortilla warmer is a round, basketlike bowl with a top that holds the tortillas and keeps them warm. You can find tortilla warmers in the housewares section of your local department store. The first time I visited my daughters in San Antonio, they took me to one of the outdoor cafés on the River Walk for lunch. I was clueless about what the tortilla warmer was for, so I just put small amounts of the taco toppings on my plate and was eating them with a fork when my daughters asked me what the heck I was doing. Then they explained the concept of filling the tortillas—that were in the tortilla warmer—with the toppings.

2 tbsp. olive oil
1 medium red onion, sliced
1 red bell pepper, cut into strips
1 green bell pepper, cut into strips
½ lb. round steak, cut into ¼" thick strips
¾ cup frozen whole kernel corn, cooked according to package directions and drained
1 jalapeño pepper, minced with seeds
½ tsp. ground cumin
½ tsp. chili powder
1½ tbsp. minced fresh cilantro
Salt and black pepper to taste
8 6" corn tortillas
1 cup shredded cheddar cheese
2 medium tomatoes, chopped
1 8 oz. container sour cream

Heat the oil in a 12" skillet over medium heat. Add the onion and bell peppers. Sauté until tender, about 10 minutes. Transfer to a plate.

Increase the heat to high. Add the steak to the skillet and stir for 1 minute, or until it is no longer pink.

Return the onion and bell peppers to the skillet. Add the corn, jalapeño, cumin, and chili powder. Stir until heated through.

Add the cilantro. Season to taste with salt and pepper. Transfer the mixture to a platter and keep warm.

Heat a separate 12" skillet over medium-high heat. Add the tortillas, one at a time, and cook on both sides. Transfer to a tortilla warmer.

Serve the steak mixture, cheese, tomatoes, and sour cream in separate bowls. Assemble the tacos and enjoy.

Serves 4

Baked Chicken Tacos

2 tbsp. olive oil
3 skinless, boneless chicken breasts, cut into 1" cubes
1 medium onion, chopped
2 14.5 oz. cans diced tomatoes, with juice
2 tsp. chili powder
1 tsp. ground cumin
½ tsp. salt
½ tsp. garlic powder
½ tsp. dried oregano
¼ tsp. ground coriander
10 8" flour tortillas, warmed
3½ cups grated queso blanco cheese*

Heat the oil in a 12" skillet over high heat. Add the chicken cubes and cook, stirring frequently, until the chicken is browned on all sides. Remove and set aside.

Reduce the heat to medium high. Add the onion and sauté until translucent.

Add the tomatoes, chili powder, cumin, salt, garlic powder, oregano, and coriander. Stir to mix. Cook, stirring frequently, until the mixture becomes very thick, about 15 minutes.

Add the chicken and stir to coat in the tomato mixture.

Preheat the oven to 450 degrees. Wrap the tortillas in plastic wrap and warm them in the microwave for 30 seconds.

Spoon equal amounts of the chicken mixture onto each tortilla and roll up tightly. Place them seam side down in a 13x9" glass baking dish. Bake for 15 minutes or until the tortillas are crisp and brown.

Remove the tacos from the oven and sprinkle the tops with the queso blanco cheese. Return to the oven and bake for 5 more minutes or until the cheese is melted.

Serves 6

*Queso blanco is a white Mexican cheese. It is sold in most large grocery stores and in Mexican markets.

Chorizo Chicken Tacos

1 to 2 tbsp. vegetable oil
4 cups ground chicken*
1½ cups chorizo sausage
1 tsp. salt
1 tsp. ground cumin
12 taco shells
3 green onions, chopped
1 cup shredded Monterey jack cheese
2 medium tomatoes, chopped
½ head of lettuce, shredded

Preheat the oven to 250 degrees.

Heat the oil in a 12" skillet over medium heat. Add the chicken, chorizo, salt, and cumin. Cook until the chicken and chorizo are cooked through, stirring frequently. Drain; return to heat.

While the chicken-chorizo mixture is cooking, warm the taco shells in the oven for 10 minutes.

Reduce the heat to medium low. Add the green onions to the chicken-chorizo mixture. Heat through, stirring occasionally.

Spoon the chicken-chorizo mixture into the warmed taco shells. Top with cheese, tomatoes, and lettuce.

Serves 6

*If you can't find ground chicken, substitute either 1 lb. ground turkey or 2 skinless, boneless chicken breasts, poached then shredded.

Shredded Chicken Tacos

2 tbsp. butter
½ cup chopped onion
2 cups finely shredded, cooked chicken breasts
1 1.25 oz. package taco seasoning mix
¼ cup water
12 taco shells, warmed
2 cups shredded lettuce
1 large tomato, chopped
1 cup shredded Monterey jack or cheddar cheese
1 8 oz. container sour cream
1 avocado, mashed
2 green onions, sliced
¼ cup black olives, chopped

Heat the butter in a 12" skillet over medium heat. Add the onion and sauté until transparent.

Stir in the chicken, taco seasoning, and water. Simmer, uncovered, for 15 minutes.

While this is cooking, warm the taco shells in the oven at 250 degrees for 10 minutes.

Spoon the chicken mixture into the taco shells. Top with lettuce, tomato, cheese, sour cream, avocado, green onions, and black olives.

Serves 6

Turkey Tomorrow Tacos

This recipe is so named because the tacos taste so much better the day after they're cooked.

1 lb. lean ground turkey breast
½ cup chopped onion
1 10 oz. can diced tomatoes with green chiles
½ tsp. ground cumin
½ tsp. chili powder
½ tsp. dried oregano
6 8" flour tortillas

Heat a 12" skillet over medium heat. Add the turkey and onion. Cook, stirring until the turkey is cooked through.

Add the tomatoes, cumin, chili powder, and oregano. Bring to a boil, then reduce the heat and cook, stirring occasionally for 5 minutes or until most of the liquid has evaporated.

Cover and refrigerate until the next day. Reheat and serve in warmed flour tortillas.

Serves 4

Chicken Tostada

Tostadas are crispy corn tortillas, similar in texture to a taco shell except they are flat. In lieu of making your own tostada, as this recipe calls for, you can buy them at the grocery store, next to the tortillas. The red corn tostadas are the best.

8 roma tomatoes, quartered
3 to 4 tbsp. olive oil, divided
Salt and black pepper to taste
8 6" corn tortillas
1 skinless, boneless chicken breast, cooked and chopped
1 medium onion, chopped
1½ cups shredded Monterey jack cheese
2 tbsp. chopped cilantro
1 large avocado, cut into 16 thin slices

Preheat the oven to 450 degrees.

Place the tomato wedges on a baking sheet. Drizzle 1 tbsp. of the olive oil over them. Season to taste with salt and black pepper. Bake for 30 minutes.

Remove the tomatoes from the oven and mash them with a fork, removing the skins. Set aside.

Brush both sides of the tortillas* with the remaining olive oil. Arrange the tortillas on a baking sheet.

Spread each tortilla with the mashed tomato. Sprinkle with the cooked chicken, then add the onion. Top with the cheese and sprinkle with the cilantro. Bake for 10 minutes or until the cheese begins to melt.

Remove from the oven and top with the avocado slices.

Serves 4

*If using store-bought tostadas, eliminate brushing the tostadas with the remaining olive oil. Just bake them in the oven, and they're good to go.

Pork Tostadas

1¼ lb. pork shoulder, cut into 1" cubes
½ tsp. salt
1 tbsp. vegetable oil
1 small onion, chopped
1 garlic clove, crushed
1 pasilla chile, seeded and ground
1 tsp. ground cinnamon
½ tsp. ground cloves
1 16 oz. can refried beans
¼ cup vegetable oil
6 6" corn tortillas
6 tbsp. sour cream
2 small tomatoes, diced
½ cup shredded Mexican Blend cheese
6 tbsp. chopped cilantro

Place the pork cubes in a medium saucepan. Cover with water and bring to a boil, then reduce the heat and simmer for 40 minutes. Drain. Shred the pork, using two forks. Place the pork in a bowl and sprinkle with the salt.

Heat 1 tbsp. oil in a 12" skillet over medium heat. Add the onion, garlic, pasilla chile, cinnamon, and cloves. Stir for 2 to 3 minutes, then add the shredded pork and cook until the meat is heated through and has absorbed the seasonings.

Heat the refried beans in the microwave or in a small saucepan over medium heat.

Heat the ¼ cup vegetable oil in a medium skillet over high heat. Add the tortillas, one at a time, turning with tongs until crisply fried. Place on paper towels to blot and absorb the excess oil.

Place the fried tortillas on individual plates. Top with the refried beans, then with the pork mixture. Add the sour cream, tomatoes, and cheese. Sprinkle with the cilantro.

Serves 6

Top Tostadas

1 16 oz. can refried beans, heated
4 6" corn tortillas, crisply fried
1 cup grated cheddar cheese
1 cup shredded lettuce, tossed with 1 tbsp. olive oil
1 large tomato, diced
1 cup guacamole
½ cup sour cream
¼ cup sliced black olives

Spread equal amounts of the refried beans on each tortilla. Sprinkle with cheese and layer on the remaining ingredients.

Serves 4

Mexican-Style Mini Pizza

1 17.3 oz. can large refrigerated flaky biscuits
½ cup thick and chunky salsa
1 12.5 oz. can cooked chicken, drained
1 15 oz. can black beans, drained and rinsed
¼ cup chopped fresh cilantro
¼ tsp. cumin
2 green onions, chopped
½ cup chopped green bell pepper
1½ cups shredded cheddar cheese
½ cup sour cream
½ cup guacamole

Preheat the oven to 350 degrees. Separate the dough into 8 biscuits. On ungreased cookie sheets, press or roll each biscuit into a 5½" circle.

Combine the salsa, chicken, black beans, cilantro, and cumin in a medium-size bowl. Mix well.

Spread the salsa mixture evenly over the biscuits to within ¼" of the edges. Top each with green onions, bell pepper, and cheese.

Bake for 20 to 25 minutes or until the biscuits are golden brown and the cheese is melted.

Spoon some of the sour cream and guacamole over the top.

Serves 4

Tex-Mex Taco Pizza

Cornmeal Crust:
1¼ cups all-purpose flour
1 package active dry yeast
¼ tsp. salt
1 cup warm water
2 tbsp. vegetable oil
¾ cup yellow cornmeal
¾ to 1¼ cups all-purpose flour

Toppings:
1 lb. lean ground beef
1 medium onion, chopped
1 green bell pepper, chopped
1 8 oz. can tomato sauce
1 2.5 oz. can sliced pitted olives, drained
1 1.25 oz. package taco seasoning mix
1 cup shredded cheddar cheese
1 cup shredded Monterey jack cheese

Preheat the oven to 425 degrees. Lightly spray two 13" pizza pans with nonstick cooking spray. Set aside.

For Cornmeal Crust: Combine 1¼ cups flour, yeast, and salt in a large mixing bowl. Add water and vegetable oil. Beat with a mixer on low speed for 30 seconds. Beat on high speed for 3 minutes.

Using a spoon, stir in the cornmeal and as much of the flour as you can.

On a lightly floured surface, knead in enough of the remaining flour to make a moderately stiff dough that is smooth and elastic (6 to 8 minutes). Divide the dough in half. Cover and let rest for 10 minutes.

On a lightly floured surface, roll each half of the dough into a circle that is 1" larger than the pizza pan.

Transfer the dough to the prepared pans. Build up the edges slightly and flute them. Prick the crusts well with a fork. Do not let the dough rise. Bake for 10 to 12 minutes or until the crusts are lightly browned.

While the crusts are cooking, prepare the toppings.

For Toppings: In a 12" skillet over medium-high heat, cook the ground beef, onion, and green bell pepper until the meat is brown and the vegetables are tender. Drain.

Stir in the tomato sauce, olives, and taco seasoning mix. Heat through.

Spread the meat mixture over the hot crusts. Sprinkle with both cheeses.

Bake for 12 minutes or until the cheese is melted and has just begun to brown.

Serves 8

Chili

Beer 'n' Black Bean Chili

San Antonio is famous for bringing chili to the world. The San Antonio "Chili Queens" operated street stands on Military Plaza in the late nineteenth century. Later, the Texas legislature made chili the official dish of the Lone Star State.

2 tbsp. olive oil
2 lb. stew beef, cut into ½" cubes
2 cups chopped onion
1 4.5 oz. can chopped green chiles
1 14.5 oz. can beef broth
1 cup beer (Dos Equis is preferred)
1 6 oz. can tomato paste
3 tbsp. chili powder
1 tsp. garlic powder
1 tsp. dried oregano
½ tsp. ground cumin
½ tsp. salt
2 15 oz. cans black beans, drained and rinsed
1 cup shredded cheddar cheese
White tortilla chips

Heat the oil in a large saucepan over medium-high heat. Add the beef and brown it on all sides.

Add the onion and sauté for 5 minutes or until it is translucent. Drain any remaining oil.

Stir in the chiles, beef broth, beer, tomato paste, chili powder, garlic powder, oregano, cumin, and salt. Bring to a boil, then reduce the heat and simmer for 1 hour to let the flavors blend, stirring occasionally.

Add the beans and simmer for 20 more minutes.

Ladle into individual serving bowls and garnish with cheddar cheese. Serve the chips on the side.

Serves 6

Corn Chip Chili

1½ lb. lean ground beef
1 medium onion, finely chopped
1 16 oz. can tomato or V-8 juice
1 16 oz. can Mexican stewed tomatoes, cut up
2 15.5 oz. cans red kidney beans, drained and rinsed
3 tbsp. chili powder (or more to taste)
¾ tsp. cumin
1 tsp. garlic powder
2 tsp. dried basil
2 tsp. dried oregano
Crushed Fritos®
1 cup shredded Mexican Blend cheese

Brown the ground beef, with the onion, over medium-high heat in a medium-size saucepan. Drain.

Add the tomato juice, stewed tomatoes, kidney beans, chili powder, cumin, garlic powder, basil, and oregano. Stir to mix, bring to a boil, then reduce the heat and simmer, covered, for 1 hour, stirring occasionally.

Ladle into individual serving bowls. Top with the crushed chips and the cheese.

Serves 6

Picante Corn Chili

1½ lb. lean ground beef
1 medium onion, finely chopped
1 garlic clove, minced
1 14.5 oz. can diced tomatoes, with liquid
½ cup picante sauce
1 8 oz. can whole kernel corn, drained
2 15.5 oz. cans pinto beans, drained and rinsed
½ tsp. cumin
1 cup water
½ cup shredded Monterey jack cheese
½ cup shredded cheddar cheese

In a medium saucepan, brown the ground beef with the onion and garlic over medium heat. Drain.

Add the tomatoes, picante sauce, corn, pinto beans, cumin, and water. Bring to a boil, then reduce the heat, cover, and simmer for 20 minutes.

Ladle into individual bowls. Top with both cheeses.

Serves 6

Crockpot Chili

Cooked in a crockpot, this chili is flavorful and is a convenient meal for a busy day. Cook the meat first in a skillet, then add all the remaining ingredients to the crockpot. When you get home, dinner will be ready.

1 lb. lean ground beef
¾ cup chopped celery
1 small onion, chopped
1 small green bell pepper, chopped
1 14.5 oz. can diced tomatoes, with juice
1 8 oz. can tomato sauce
2 tbsp. tomato paste
1 15.5 oz. can red kidney beans, drained and rinsed
1 4.5 oz. can green chiles, drained, seeded, and chopped
½ tsp. marjoram
¼ tsp. garlic powder
1 bay leaf

Brown the ground beef in a 12" skillet over high heat. Drain.

Transfer to a crockpot. Add all the remaining ingredients. Stir to mix. Cook on low for 8 hours. Remove bay leaf before serving.

Serves 6

Green Chile Chili

Chili is usually cooked with beef, beans, peppers, and a tomato-based sauce, though there's a hot debate about whether true chili should have beans. Chili is also referred to as a bowl of red. A chile is a hot, dried pepper. The plural of chile is chiles.

1 lb. lean ground beef
1 lb. stew beef, cubed
1 green bell pepper, chopped
1 large onion, chopped
1 4.5 oz. can chopped green chiles
1 8 oz. can tomato sauce
2 14.5 oz. cans diced tomatoes, with juice
2 15.5 oz. cans red kidney beans, drained and rinsed
3 tbsp. chili powder
½ tsp. salt
½ tsp. cinnamon
½ tsp. cumin
½ tsp. oregano
½ tsp. garlic powder
¼ tsp. cloves
¼ tsp. black pepper

Brown the ground beef and the stew beef with the green bell pepper and onion in a large saucepan over medium-high heat. Drain.

Add the chiles, tomato sauce, diced tomatoes, beans, chili powder, salt, cinnamon, cumin, oregano, garlic powder, cloves, and black pepper. Stir to mix. Bring to a boil, then reduce the heat and simmer, covered, for 2 hours or until the stew beef is tender, stirring occasionally.

Serves 6

Slow-Simmered Chunky Chili

2 lb. beef stew meat, cut in small chunks
1 large onion, chopped
2 garlic cloves, chopped
1 28 oz. can whole tomatoes, with juice
2 8 oz. cans tomato sauce
2 15.5 oz. cans pinto beans, drained and rinsed
1 4.5 oz. can chopped green chiles
1½ tsp. salt
2 tbsp. chili powder
½ tsp. cayenne pepper
1 tsp. dried oregano

Heat a large saucepan over medium heat. Rinse the meat under cold running water and add to the pan. Brown the meat in its own juices. About halfway through browning, add the onion and garlic. Sauté until tender.

Add the tomatoes, tomato sauce, beans, chiles, salt, chili powder, cayenne pepper, and oregano. Stir to mix. Bring to a boil, then reduce the heat and simmer for 2 hours, stirring occasionally.

Serves 6

Tortilla Chili

1 lb. lean ground beef
1 tbsp. minced garlic
1 green bell pepper, chopped
1 medium onion, finely chopped
1 14.5 oz. can diced tomatoes, with juice
1 6 oz. can tomato paste
1 cup water, more if necessary
3 tbsp. chili powder, or to taste
Celery salt and black pepper to taste
4 6" flour tortillas, cut up
1 15.5 oz. can kidney beans, drained and rinsed
Shredded cheddar cheese
Sour cream

Brown the meat in a medium saucepan with the garlic, green bell pepper, and onion. Drain.

Add the tomatoes, tomato paste, water, chili powder, celery salt, and black pepper. Stir to mix. Bring to a boil, then reduce the heat, cover, and simmer for 45 minutes.

Add the tortillas and beans. Simmer for 15 more minutes.

Ladle into individual bowls. Top with the cheddar cheese and a dollop of sour cream.

Serves 6

Variations: For **Chicken Tortilla Chili**, add 2 skinless, boneless chicken breasts, cut up and browned in 2 tbsp. olive oil instead of the beef. To make **Chicken Salsa Chili**, add 2 cups salsa instead of the diced tomatoes.

Chorizo Chili

This chili should come with a warning. It's very spicy and is not for people with timid taste buds.

1 lb. chorizo sausage
2 cups chopped onion
2 cups water
1½ tsp. chili powder
1½ tsp. dried oregano
1½ tsp. ground cumin
1 tsp. salt
¼ tsp. crushed red pepper
2 14.5 oz. cans stewed tomatoes, with juice
1 15.5 oz. can black-eyed peas, drained and rinsed
1 4.5 oz. can chopped green chiles
2 garlic cloves, minced
1 cup shredded cheddar cheese
½ cup sour cream
1 medium tomato, diced

Place the chorizo and onion in a large saucepan. Cook over medium heat until the sausage is browned and the onion is tender. Drain.

Add the water, chili powder, oregano, cumin, salt, crushed red pepper, stewed tomatoes, black-eyed peas, green chiles, and garlic. Stir well. Bring to a boil, then reduce the heat and simmer for 1 hour, stirring occasionally.

Ladle into individual serving bowls. Sprinkle with cheese and place a dollop of sour cream in the center. Top with diced tomatoes.

Serves 6

Pinto Chorizo Chili

¾ lb. lean ground beef
¾ lb. chorizo
1½ cups chopped onion
2 14.5 oz. cans diced tomatoes, with juice
1 tbsp. chili powder
2 15.5 oz. cans pinto beans, drained and rinsed

Brown the ground beef and chorizo with the onion in a saucepan over medium heat. Drain.

Add the tomatoes, chili powder, and beans. Bring to a boil, then reduce the heat, cover, and simmer for 1 hour, stirring occasionally.

Serves 6

Paseo Del Rio Chili

You can expect to find this chili at any of the restaurants on the River Walk.

2 to 3 tbsp. olive oil
2 cups chopped onion
2 lb. lean pork, cubed
1 lb. lean ground beef
2 garlic cloves, minced
¼ cup chili powder
1 tbsp. ground cumin
2 tsp. dried oregano
2 14.5 oz. cans diced tomatoes
1 14.5 oz. can beef broth
1 12 oz. can beer, or substitute 1½ cups tomato juice
1 4.5 oz. can chopped green chiles
2 15.5 oz. cans pinto beans, rinsed and drained
Salt and black pepper to taste
Shredded cheddar cheese
Freshly chopped cilantro
White tortilla chips

Heat the oil in a large skillet over medium heat. Add the onion and sauté until tender.

Add the pork and ground beef. Cook until brown. Drain.

Stir in the garlic, chili powder, cumin, and oregano. Cook for 5 minutes.

Add the tomatoes, broth, beer, and green chiles. Stir well. Bring to a boil, then reduce the heat and simmer, covered, for 1½ hours, or until the pork is tender, stirring occasionally.

Add the pinto beans and cook, uncovered, for 10 minutes or until the sauce thickens. Season to taste with salt and pepper.

Ladle into individual serving bowls. Sprinkle with the cheese and cilantro. Tuck a few tortilla chips in around the side of the bowl.

Serves 6

Chicken Cannellini Chili

This white bean chili is lightning hot.

1 tbsp. vegetable oil
4 skinless, boneless chicken breasts, cut into bite-size pieces
1 medium onion, chopped
1 garlic clove, minced
1 14.5 oz. can chicken broth
2 15.5 oz. cans cannellini beans, rinsed and drained
1 15.5 oz. can cannellini beans, rinsed, drained, and mashed
1 4.5 oz. can chopped green chiles, with juice
½ tsp. salt
1 tsp. ground cumin
½ tsp. dried oregano
½ tsp. chili powder
¼ tsp. black pepper
⅛ tsp. cayenne pepper
½ cup shredded Monterey jack cheese
½ cup sour cream
Chopped fresh cilantro

Heat the oil in a large saucepan over medium-high heat. Add the chicken, onion, and garlic. Sauté until the chicken is brown and the onion is tender.

Stir in the chicken broth, beans, green chiles, salt, cumin, oregano, chili powder, black pepper, and cayenne pepper. Bring to a boil, then reduce the heat and simmer, uncovered, for 45 minutes.

Ladle into individual serving bowls. Sprinkle with the Monterey jack cheese and add a dollop or two of sour cream. Sprinkle with cilantro.

Serves 6

Chicken Chili

3 tbsp. olive oil, divided
1 medium onion, chopped
1 green bell pepper, chopped
½ cup chopped button mushrooms
2 skinless, boneless chicken breasts, chopped
3 tbsp. chili powder
1 tsp. cumin
½ tsp. oregano
3 garlic cloves, minced
1 15.5 oz. can red kidney beans, drained and rinsed
1 14.5 oz. can diced tomatoes, with juice
1 8 oz. can tomato sauce
1 4.5 oz. can diced green chiles
Salt and black pepper to taste
1 cup shredded cheddar cheese
Tortilla chips, or cornbread

Heat 1 tbsp. of the oil in a large saucepan over medium heat. Add the onion, green bell pepper, and mushrooms. Sauté for 5 minutes or until the vegetables are tender. Remove and set aside.

Add the remaining oil to the saucepan and turn the heat to high. Add the chicken and brown on all sides. Drain any remaining oil.

Return the reserved vegetables to the saucepan. Add the chili powder, cumin, oregano, and garlic. Stir to season the chicken and vegetables.

Add the beans, diced tomatoes, tomato sauce, and green chiles. Stir to mix. Bring to a boil, then reduce the heat, cover, and simmer for 1 to 1½ hours, stirring occasionally. Season to taste with salt and pepper.

Ladle into individual serving bowls and garnish with the cheddar cheese. Serve with tortilla chips or cornbread.

Serves 6

Chipotle Chicken Chili

Soaking the dried chipotle peppers with the beans gives them a nice, smoky flavor.

2 cups dry black beans
8 cups water
2 chipotle peppers
3 bay leaves
2 tbsp. vegetable oil
3 skinless, boneless chicken breasts, chopped
1 large onion, chopped
3 garlic cloves, minced
2 green bell peppers, chopped
1½ tsp. salt
½ tsp. black pepper
1 tbsp. chili powder
1 tbsp. cumin
1 14.5 oz. can chicken broth
Sour cream

Place the beans in a large saucepan with the water, chipotle peppers, and bay leaves. Bring to a boil, then reduce the heat to low. Cover and simmer for 1 hour or until the beans are tender, stirring occasionally.

Remove the chipotle peppers, chop, and set aside. Discard the bay leaves.

Heat the oil in a large, heavy stockpot over medium-high heat. Add the chicken and brown on all sides. Remove and set aside.

Reduce the heat to medium. Add the onion, garlic, green bell peppers, salt, and black pepper. Sauté until the vegetables are tender.

Return the chicken to the pan. Stir in the chili powder, cumin, and reserved chipotle peppers. Stir to mix. Cook, stirring frequently, for 3 minutes.

Stir in the black beans with their liquid and add the chicken broth. Bring to a boil, then reduce the heat and simmer for 45 minutes or until the flavors have blended and the chili is thickened.

Ladle into individual serving bowls and top with a dollop of sour cream.

Serves 6

Pinto Chicken Chili

Pinto beans are the preferred bean in a bowl of chili.

2 to 3 tbsp. olive oil
4 skinless, boneless chicken breasts, cubed
1 green bell pepper, chopped
1 large onion, chopped
3 jalapeño peppers, seeded and chopped
3 garlic cloves, minced
¼ cup sun-dried tomatoes
2 tbsp. chili powder
1 tbsp. ground cumin
2 tsp. dried oregano
2 cups chicken broth
1 cup dried pinto beans, soaked overnight in water, drained
1 large tomato, chopped
1 cup fresh or frozen corn
Salt and black pepper to taste

Heat the oil in a large saucepan over medium heat. Add the chicken and brown on all sides.

Add the green bell pepper, onion, jalapeños, and garlic. Sauté until tender.

Add the sun-dried tomatoes, chili powder, cumin, and oregano. Stir well and cook for 2 to 3 minutes.

Add the broth and beans. Stir to mix. Bring to a boil, then reduce the heat and simmer, uncovered, for 1 to 1½ hours, stirring occasionally.

Add the tomato and corn. Continue to simmer for 30 more minutes or until the beans are tender. Season to taste with salt and black pepper.

Serves 6

Enchiladas

Beef Enchiladas

1 lb. lean ground beef
1 small onion
¼ tsp. ground cumin
1½ tsp. chili powder
2 10 oz. cans enchilada sauce
¼ cup vegetable oil
10 6" corn tortillas
2 cups shredded Monterey jack cheese, divided

Preheat the oven to 350 degrees. Lightly spray a 13x9" baking dish with nonstick cooking spray. Set aside.

In a medium-size saucepan, brown the ground beef with the onion over medium-high heat. Season with cumin and chili powder while the meat is cooking. (If you season the meat while it is cooking, there is no need to drain it because the fat evaporates.)

Place ½ cup of the enchilada sauce in a shallow pie pan and set aside.

Add the oil to a 12" skillet and heat for 2 minutes over medium heat. Using tongs, fry each tortilla, one at a time, for 3 seconds on each side. Place on paper towels to drain, then stack on a separate plate.

One at a time, dip each tortilla on both sides in the enchilada sauce. Place the dipped tortillas on a separate plate.

Fill each tortilla with the beef mixture and cheese. Roll up tightly. Place seam side down in the prepared baking dish. Top with the remaining enchilada sauce and sprinkle with the cheese. Cover with aluminum foil and bake for 30 minutes.

Uncover and bake for 5 to 10 more minutes to brown the cheese.

Serves 6

Saucy Beef Enchiladas

⅓ cup flour
1 cup milk
1½ cups beef broth
1 lb. lean ground beef
1½ tsp. cumin
½ tsp. chili powder
Salt and black pepper to taste
1 7 oz. can diced green chiles
½ cup chopped green onion
1 cup sour cream
8 7" flour tortillas, warmed
¼ cup grated cheddar cheese

Preheat the oven to 350 degrees. Lightly spray a 13x9" baking dish with nonstick cooking spray. Set aside.

In a small bowl, whisk together the flour and milk.

Pour the mixture into a medium-size saucepan and add the broth. Bring to a boil, stirring. Let cook for 5 minutes. Remove the pan from the heat and set aside.

Brown the ground beef in a 12" skillet over medium-high heat. Drain.

Reduce the heat to medium low. Add half of the sauce and the cumin, chili powder, salt, pepper, chiles, green onion, and sour cream. Heat through.

Warm the tortillas in the microwave for 30 seconds to make them soft and pliable.

Spread each tortilla with ½ cup of the meat sauce and a spoonful of cheese. Roll up and place seam side down in the prepared baking dish. Pour the remaining sauce and any remaining meat mixture over the filled tortillas, being sure that all are covered with the sauce. Bake for 20 minutes.

Remove from the oven and sprinkle with cheese. Return to the oven for 10 more minutes to melt the cheese.

Serves 4

Enticing Enchiladas

You can easily substitute chicken for beef in this recipe.

2 to 3 tbsp. butter
1 small white onion, chopped
3 green onions, chopped
½ tsp. garlic powder
½ tsp. seasoned salt
1 7 oz. can chopped green chiles
2 8 oz. packages cream cheese, softened
2 cups cooked beef, diced or shredded (any cut of beef will do)
8 8" flour tortillas, warmed
2 10 oz. cans enchilada sauce
1 16 oz. package shredded Monterey jack cheese

Preheat the oven to 350 degrees. Lightly spray a 13x9" baking dish with nonstick cooking spray. Set aside.

Melt the butter in a 12" skillet over medium heat. Add the white and green onions. Sauté until tender and translucent.

Reduce the heat to low. Add the garlic powder, seasoned salt, and green chiles. Stir in the cream cheese. Cook, stirring, until the cream cheese is melted.

Add the cooked beef. Stir to mix. Heat through.

Put 3 heaping spoonfuls of the beef mixture on each tortilla. Roll up and place seam side down in the prepared baking dish.

Pour the enchilada sauce over, then sprinkle the cheese on the top. Bake, uncovered, for 35 minutes.

Serves 6

Enchilada Stack

In this recipe, instead of rolling the tortillas, layer them.

½ lb. lean ground beef
1 8 oz. can tomato sauce
½ cup water
1½ tsp. chili powder
¼ tsp. ground cumin
4 6" flour tortillas
¼ cup finely chopped onion
3 tbsp. finely chopped jalapeño pepper
1 cup shredded cheddar cheese

Preheat the oven to 350 degrees. Lightly spray a 1½-qt. round casserole dish with nonstick cooking spray. Set aside.

In a medium-size saucepan, brown the ground beef over medium-high heat. Drain.

Stir in the tomato sauce, water, chili powder, and cumin. Bring to a boil, then reduce the heat and simmer for 15 minutes.

While this is cooking, tightly wrap the stack of tortillas in aluminum foil and bake for 15 to 20 minutes or until soft and pliable.

Place one of the tortillas in the prepared casserole dish. Layer one-quarter each of the meat mixture, onion, jalapeño, and cheese. Repeat three times.

Cover with aluminum foil and bake for 15 minutes. Uncover and bake for 5 to 10 more minutes to brown the cheese.

Serves 4

Fiesta Beef Enchiladas

1 cup water
2 tbsp. picante sauce
12 6" corn tortillas
2 lb. lean ground beef
1 medium onion, chopped
1 tsp. salt
⅛ tsp. black pepper
2 tsp. ground cumin
1 tbsp. chili powder
1 tsp. garlic powder
¾ cup black olives, sliced
¼ cup picante sauce
8 tbsp. butter
2 tbsp. all-purpose flour
1½ cups milk
1 16 oz. container sour cream
2 cups shredded cheddar cheese

Preheat the oven to 375 degrees. Lightly spray a 13x9" baking dish with nonstick cooking spray. Set aside.

Combine the water and 2 tbsp. picante sauce in a large shallow dish. Place the tortillas in the picante sauce mixture. Let stand for 5 minutes. Drain.

Cook the ground beef and onion in a 12" skillet over medium heat until brown. Drain.

Stir in the salt, pepper, cumin, chili powder, garlic powder, olives, and ¼ cup picante sauce. Reduce the heat and simmer for 5 minutes.

Melt the butter in a small skillet over low heat. Add the flour, stirring for 1 minute or until smooth.

Raise the heat to medium. Gradually add the milk, stirring constantly, until thickened and bubbly.

Remove the pan from the heat. Add the sour cream and stir until well blended.

Place half of the tortillas in the prepared baking dish. Pour half of the sour cream sauce over the tortillas, then spoon half of the meat mixture evenly over the sauce. Sprinkle half of the cheese over the meat mixture. Repeat.

Place in the oven and bake for 25 minutes.

Serves 6

Chorizo Enchiladas

Serve these enchiladas with a side of rice and beans, chopped lettuce and tomato, and sour cream.

1 lb. chorizo sausage
1 medium onion, diced
1 8 oz. package cream cheese, cubed
8 6" corn tortillas, warmed
1 8 oz. package Monterey jack cheese, divided
1 10 oz. can enchilada sauce, divided

Preheat the oven to 350 degrees. Lightly spray a 13x9" baking dish with nonstick cooking spray. Set aside.

Cook the chorizo with the onion in a 12" skillet over medium-high heat. Drain. Remove the pan from the heat and stir in the cream cheese.

Fill each tortilla with the chorizo-cream-cheese mixture and Monterey jack cheese. Roll up. Place seam side down in the sauce in the baking dish.

Pour the enchilada sauce over. Sprinkle with the remaining cheese. Cover with aluminum foil and bake for 25 minutes. Remove the foil and return to the oven for 5 minutes to brown the cheese.

Serves 4

Variation: To make **Chorizo Bean Enchiladas**, add 1 16-oz. can refried beans to the cooked chorizo.

Pork Enchiladas with Tomatillo Sauce

1¼ lb. pork shoulder, diced
2 tbsp. vegetable oil
1 medium onion, finely chopped
2 garlic cloves, crushed
2 serrano peppers, stemmed, seeded, and finely chopped
2 cups drained canned tomatillos
6 6" corn tortillas, warmed
¾ cup grated Mexican Blend cheese

Add the diced pork to a medium-size saucepan and cover with water. Bring to a boil, then reduce the heat and simmer for 40 minutes. Drain, let cool, then shred with two forks.

Preheat the oven to 350 degrees. Lightly spray a 13x9" baking dish with nonstick cooking spray. Set aside.

Heat the oil in a 12" skillet over medium heat. Add the onion and garlic. Cook for 3 to 4 minutes.

Add the serrano peppers and the tomatillos. Cook, stirring constantly, until the tomatillos begin to break up. Reduce the heat and simmer for 10 more minutes. Let cool slightly, then purée in a blender.

Spoon equal amounts of the shredded pork on the center of each tortilla and roll it up. Place it seam side down in the prepared baking dish.

Pour the sauce over. Sprinkle with cheese. Bake for 25 to 30 minutes or until the cheese bubbles.

Serves 4

Cheese Enchiladas

The whole family gets together almost every Saturday for dinner. My daughter, Jennifer, loves cheese, so when it's her turn to cook, which she doesn't love, she sometimes makes these cheese enchiladas. Rice and beans, along with chopped lettuce and tomato, are served on the side, and my youngest daughter, Jaime, makes her great guacamole (page 25).

2 10 oz. cans enchilada sauce*
¼ cup vegetable oil
12 6" red corn tortillas
3 cups shredded Monterey jack cheese, divided

Preheat the oven to 350 degrees. Pour ½ cup of the sauce into a 13x9" baking dish. Set aside. Place ½ cup of the enchilada sauce in a shallow pie pan and set aside.

Add the oil to a 12" skillet and heat for 2 minutes over medium heat. Using tongs, fry each tortilla, one at a time, for 3 seconds on each side. Place on paper towels to drain, then stack on a separate plate.

One at a time, dip each tortilla on both sides in the enchilada sauce. Place the dipped tortillas on a separate plate.

Generously fill each tortilla with the cheese. Roll up tightly. Place seam side down in the prepared baking dish. Top with the remaining enchilada sauce and sprinkle, again generously, with the cheese. Bake for 20 minutes or until the cheese is melted.

Serves 6

*If you can find it, use 2 16-oz. jars of Sydney's Enchilada Sauce (mild heat level). It's available in San Antonio at the Central Market H-E-B. You can order it online at www.sydneysgourmet.net.

Cheesy Chicken Enchiladas

1¼ lb. deli chicken breast, sliced 3½" thick and cut into ½" cubes
1 lb. Monterey jack cheese with jalapeño, shredded and divided
1 8 oz. container sour cream
1 tsp. chili powder
¼ tsp. cayenne pepper
10 6" flour tortillas, warmed
1 19 oz. can enchilada sauce, divided
½ cup sliced black olives
¼ cup chopped green onion

Preheat the oven to 350 degrees.

In a medium-size bowl, combine the chicken, 1½ cups cheese, sour cream, chili powder, and cayenne pepper. Mix well.

Place ¼ cup of the chicken mixture on each tortilla. Roll up to enclose the filling.

Pour ½ cup of the enchilada sauce onto the bottom of a 13x9" baking dish. Arrange the tortillas seam side down in the baking dish.

Top with the remaining enchilada sauce and cheese. Bake for 20 minutes or until heated through.

To serve, top the enchiladas with the olives and green onion.

Serves 6

Substitution: Use deli mesquite turkey instead of chicken.

Chicken Chipotle Enchiladas

1 cup chopped green onion
1½ cups shredded Mexican Blend cheese
2 skinless, boneless chicken breasts, cooked and shredded
1 16 oz. jar chipotle salsa
¼ cup vegetable oil
12 6" corn tortillas

Preheat the oven to 350 degrees. Lightly spray a 13x9" baking dish with nonstick cooking spray. Set aside.

In a medium-size bowl, combine the green onion, cheese, and chicken. Mix well.

Place the chipotle salsa in a shallow pie pan and set aside.

Add the oil to a 12" skillet and heat for 2 minutes over medium heat. Using tongs, fry each tortilla, one at a time, for 3 seconds on each side. Place on paper towels to drain, then stack on a separate plate.

One at a time, dip each tortilla on both sides in the salsa. Place the dipped tortillas on a separate plate.

Spread ½ cup of the chicken mixture on each tortilla. Roll up tightly. Place the tortillas, seam side down, in the prepared baking dish. Top the enchiladas with the remaining chicken mixture and salsa. Bake for 20 minutes.

Serves 6

Chicken Enchiladas

1 16 oz. container sour cream, divided
1 7 oz. can diced green chiles
4 green onions, chopped
½ cup chopped fresh cilantro
1½ tsp. ground cumin
2 cups diced, cooked chicken
1 8 oz. package grated sharp cheddar cheese, divided
10 8" flour tortillas, warmed
1 8 oz. package cream cheese, cut lengthwise into 10 strips
1½ 16 oz. cans enchilada sauce

Preheat the oven to 350 degrees. Lightly spray a 13x9" baking dish with nonstick cooking spray. Set aside.

In a large bowl, combine 1¾ cups of the sour cream, chiles, green onions, cilantro, and cumin. Mix in the chicken and ½ cup cheddar cheese.

Place ½ cup of this mixture in the center of each tortilla. Add a cream cheese strip. Roll up to enclose the filling. Arrange seam side down in the prepared baking dish.

Pour the enchilada sauce over the tortillas. Cover with aluminum foil and bake for 45 minutes or until the sauce bubbles and the enchiladas are heated through.

Remove from the oven and uncover. Sprinkle with the remaining cheddar cheese. Return to the oven and bake until the cheese melts and begins to brown.

To serve, top enchiladas with a dollop of sour cream.

Serves 6

Chicken Enchiladas Rancheras

Flor Maria and Gonzolo Pozo, owners of the Picante Grill (www.picantegrill.com), make the best ranchera sauce in town according to their customers. Flor suggests making a double or triple batch of the salsa to use for Huevos Rancheros or on charbroiled steak for Bistec Ranchero. Actually, it's good with just about everything.

2 skinless, boneless chicken breasts
2 qt. water
1 tsp. salt
1 garlic clove
½ carrot
1 thick slice onion
1 stalk celery
1 tbsp. butter
2 large onions, thinly sliced
1 bay leaf
½ tsp. oregano
1 small jalapeño pepper, thinly sliced (include seeds for a hot salsa, remove for a mild salsa)
1 large clove garlic, finely chopped
4 medium tomatoes, thinly sliced
1 tsp. salt
8 6" white corn tortillas
2 cups shredded Monterey jack cheese

Combine the chicken breasts, water, salt, garlic, carrot, onion, and celery in a heavy pot. Bring to a boil, then reduce the heat and simmer until the chicken is tender, 15 to 20 minutes.

Remove the chicken and let it cool for 10 minutes, then shred it with two forks. Set aside.

Strain 2 cups of the poaching liquid and reserve it.

Melt the butter in a 12" skillet over medium-high heat. Add the onions, bay leaf, and oregano. Sauté until the onions are translucent, about 5 minutes.

Add the jalapeño and sauté for 1 more minute, stirring.

Stir in the garlic and tomatoes.

Add the salt and the reserved chicken broth. Reduce the heat to low and let the sauce reduce until it thickens slightly, 15 to 20 minutes. Remove the bay leaf.

Preheat the broiler.

Spray each tortilla with vegetable oil spray on both sides. Stack them on a plate and cover with plastic wrap. Microwave on high for 30 seconds to make the tortillas soft and pliable.

Fill the tortillas with the shredded chicken, then roll them up.

Place the filled tortillas in a 13x9" baking dish, seam side down. Cover with the sauce mixture and top generously with cheese.

Place the dish under the broiler for several minutes. Remove when the cheese is melted and begins to bubble.

Serves 6

Variation: To make **Cheese Enchiladas Rancheros**, omit the chicken. Stuff the tortillas with a mixture of Monterey jack and cheddar cheeses. Use canned chicken broth to make the sauce.

Easy Chicken Enchiladas

1 12.5 oz. can chunk white chicken, drained
1½ cups shredded cheddar cheese, divided
1 4.5 oz. can chopped green chiles, drained
¼ cup green onion, chopped
1 10 oz. can enchilada sauce, divided
8 6" corn tortillas, warmed

Preheat the oven to 350 degrees.

In a medium-size bowl, combine the chicken, 1 cup cheese, green chiles, and onion. Mix well.

Spread half of the enchilada sauce in the bottom of a 13x9" baking dish. Set aside.

Spread equal amounts of the chicken mixture into each tortilla. Roll up. Place seam side down in the sauce in the baking dish.

Pour the remaining sauce over. Sprinkle with the remaining cheese. Cover with aluminum foil and bake for 25 minutes.

Serves 4

Enchiladas Verdes

Sarah Lucero, a native San Antonian and anchor for KENS-TV, cherishes her Hispanic heritage, which has enriched her life with its traditions, food, faith, and love of family. Luckily, her mother and grandmother have passed along the delicious Mexican recipes that the family has enjoyed for generations. Hope you enjoy, too!

1 whole chicken, cut up
5 garlic cloves, divided
1 medium white or yellow onion, quartered, divided
1 poblano pepper, stem and seeds removed, cut into length-wide slices
3 tbsp. salt
8 to 10 tomatillos, peeled and quartered
2 cups water
¼ to ½ cup canola cooking oil
18 to 20 corn tortillas
1½ cups shredded white Mexican cheese
Sour cream, for garnish

Fill a large stockpot half full with water. Place the chicken, 3 garlic cloves, ½ white or yellow onion, poblano pepper slices, and salt into the stockpot. Make sure the water covers all of the chicken.

Over medium heat, bring to a boil for 30 to 45 minutes or until the chicken is cooked through.

While this is cooking, place the tomatillos in a separate saucepan with 2 cups water, the remaining 2 garlic cloves, and the remaining ½ onion. Cook on low to medium heat for 30 to 45 minutes. When the tomatillos have softened, begin to mash them with a potato masher.

Remove the tomatillo mixture and blend for 30 seconds in a blender. Season to taste with salt.

Remove the chicken from the water. Now for the fun part—deboning the chicken! This is a tedious process, but homemade chicken is so much better than precooked chicken breasts. (However, precooked chicken can be substituted.)

After deboning the chicken, remove the fat and the skin. Shred with two forks, then bathe the chicken in some of its own broth and ½ to ¾ cup blended tomatillo sauce.

Place about ¼ cup cooking oil in a large, 2" deep skillet, over low heat.

Run about 4 corn tortillas at a time under the faucet, then place the wet tortillas on a paper towel in the microwave for 25 seconds on high power.

Dip the tortillas in the hot oil to coat them lightly. (My mom used to dip them in a deep fryer, but my version uses less oil.)

Place the tortillas flat, one at a time, into a 13x9" baking dish. Fill each with chicken, then roll up and place seam side down. Pour the tomatillo sauce over the enchiladas, then sprinkle with cheese.

You can either microwave them to melt the cheese or place into a 350-degree oven for a few minutes.

Use a spatula to scoop the enchiladas out of the baking dish. If you like, top each enchilada with a spoonful of sour cream. Serve with beans and rice or just a salad, if you're trying to be good.

Serves 10

Creamy Chicken Enchiladas

1 cup water
1 chicken bouillon cube
2 bay leaves
¼ tsp. black pepper
¼ tsp. chili powder
¼ tsp. oregano
2 skinless, boneless chicken breasts
2 to 3 tbsp. butter
1 cup chopped onion
1 garlic clove, minced
1 4.5 oz. can chopped green chiles, drained
1 15 oz. can black beans, drained and rinsed
1 tsp. ground cumin
1 8 oz. package cream cheese, cut into chunks
8 6" flour tortillas, warmed
1 10 oz. can enchilada sauce
1 cup shredded cheddar cheese

Pour the water into a medium-size saucepan. Add the bouillon cube, bay leaves, black pepper, chili powder, and oregano. Bring to a simmer. Add the chicken and poach for 10 minutes, turning chicken occasionally. Discard the bay leaves. Remove the chicken and shred with two forks or chop into small pieces. Set aside. (Reserve the chicken broth for another use.)

Preheat the oven to 350 degrees. Lightly spray a 13x9" baking dish with nonstick cooking spray. Set aside.

Heat a 10" skillet over medium heat. Add the butter. When it sizzles, add the onion and sauté for 2 to 3 minutes.

Add the garlic and green chiles to the skillet. Sauté for 2 to 3 more minutes, stirring occasionally.

Add the beans, chicken, cumin, and cream cheese. Stir to mix. Heat through, but do not boil.

Spoon ⅓ cup mixture onto each tortilla and roll up.

Arrange the tortillas in the prepared baking dish. Pour the enchilada sauce over and sprinkle with cheese. Cover with aluminum foil and bake for 25 minutes. Uncover and bake for 5 more minutes to brown the cheese.

Serves 4

Beef and Pork

Best Brisket

Texans love brisket. Cooked long and slow, the meat becomes very tender. Brisket is usually cooked in a barbecue smoker, but this recipe lets you cook it in the oven.

1 6 lb. trimmed brisket
⅓ cup liquid smoke
2 tsp. onion powder
2 tsp. garlic powder
2 tsp. celery salt
1 tbsp. Worcestershire sauce
Salt and black pepper to taste
¾ cup barbeque sauce

Place the brisket in a broiler pan. Pour the liquid smoke over the brisket, then sprinkle with onion powder, garlic powder, and celery salt. Cover with aluminum foil and refrigerate overnight.

When ready to cook, preheat the oven to 275 degrees. Remove the aluminum foil and sprinkle on the Worcestershire sauce. Season with salt and pepper.

Place in the oven and cook for 5 hours.

Remove the brisket from the oven and spread on the barbeque sauce. Return it to the oven and cook for 1 more hour.

Serves 8

Alamo City Pot Roast

It can get a little cool in San Antonio during the winter. This juicy pot roast is a hearty meal with a nice kick that will warm you on the inside. If you want an even bigger kick, use a jalapeño pepper instead of the poblano.

2 lb. rump roast
1¾ tsp. salt
3 garlic cloves, pressed
¼ tsp. dried oregano
½ tsp. chili powder
⅛ tsp. ground black pepper
1 tbsp. olive oil
2 to 3 tbsp. vegetable oil
1 tomato, coarsely chopped
1 onion, coarsely chopped
1 green bell pepper, coarsely chopped
1 poblano pepper, finely chopped
10 black olives, pitted and chopped
2 tsp. capers
⅓ cup tomato sauce
2½ cups beef broth
6 medium red potatoes, peeled and quartered

Rub the meat with the salt, then with the garlic, oregano, chili powder, black pepper, and olive oil. Place the meat in a bowl and cover with plastic wrap. Marinate in the refrigerator for 30 minutes to 2 hours, turning occasionally.

Heat the vegetable oil over medium-high heat in a Dutch oven. Brown the meat, then remove and set aside.

Discard all but 2 tbsp. oil from the pan. Reduce the heat to medium low. Add the tomato, onion, green bell pepper, and poblano pepper. Sauté for 5 minutes.

Add the olives, capers, and tomato sauce. Cook for 5 more minutes.

Return the meat to the pan. Add the beef broth and bring to a boil. Reduce the heat, cover, and simmer for 1½ hours.

Add the potatoes. Simmer for 30 more minutes or until the meat and potatoes are tender and the sauce has thickened.

Serve on a platter with the vegetables on the side.

Serves 6

Beef Fajitas

What could be better than a hot plate of sizzling fajitas served with guacamole and salsa?

4 garlic cloves, mashed to a paste
1 tsp. salt
¼ cup fresh lime juice
1½ tsp. ground cumin
2 tbsp. olive oil
2 lb. skirt steak, trimmed and cut into large pieces
2 tbsp. vegetable oil
1 red bell pepper, sliced
1 green bell pepper, sliced
1 yellow bell pepper, sliced
1 large red onion, sliced
2 garlic cloves, minced
Garlic butter (optional)*
12 8" flour tortillas, warmed
Guacamole
Salsa

In a large bowl, whisk together the garlic, salt, lime juice, cumin, and olive oil.

Add the steak to the marinade, turning to coat it. Cover the bowl and let the steak marinate in the refrigerator for at least 1 hour.

When ready to cook, grill or broil the steak to desired doneness. Transfer to a cutting board and let rest for 10 minutes.

While the meat is resting, heat the 2 tbsp. vegetable oil in a 12" skillet over high heat. Add the bell peppers, onion, and garlic. Cook, stirring, for 5 minutes or until the peppers are softened.

Slice the steak thin across the grain on the diagonal. Arrange the steak slices on a platter with the bell peppers and onion. Drizzle any steak juices over the steak. Drizzle the garlic butter over the steak and peppers.

Fill warmed tortillas with steak, peppers, guacamole, and salsa.

Serves 6

*To make the garlic butter, melt 6 tbsp. butter in a small saucepan. Add 2 tsp. garlic powder. Stir until dissolved.

Green Chile Meatballs

This is the Tex-Mex version of spaghetti and meatballs.

1 lb. lean ground beef
½ cup breadcrumbs
2 tbsp. finely chopped cilantro
½ cup minced onion
Pinch of salt and black pepper
3 to 4 tbsp. olive oil
3 cups water, divided
3 tbsp. chopped chives
½ cup finely sliced green onion
2 garlic cloves, minced
2 tsp. beef bouillon
1 14.5 oz. can diced tomatoes, with juice
Salt and black pepper to taste
1 4.5 oz. can chopped green chiles
2 cups cooked white rice, hot

Place the ground beef, breadcrumbs, cilantro, onion, salt, and pepper into a medium-size bowl. Shape into small meatballs.

Heat the olive oil in a 12" skillet over medium-high heat. Add the meatballs and thoroughly brown on all sides. Reduce the heat to low, add ½ cup water, cover, and let steam for 10 minutes. Remove meatballs and set aside.

Add the remaining water to the skillet, stirring to scrape up the flavorful brown bits from the bottom of the skillet.

Add the chives, green onion, garlic, beef bouillon, and tomatoes. Bring to a boil, then reduce the heat and simmer for 10 minutes. Season to taste with salt and pepper.

Return the meatballs to the skillet. Add the chiles and simmer for 30 more minutes.

Serve over a bed of hot rice.

Serves 4

Rippin' Good Round Steak

You might recognize this dish as a variation on a Chinese recipe that uses soy sauce instead of enchilada sauce.

⅓ cup all-purpose flour
Salt and black pepper to taste
1 tsp. cumin
2 lb. round steak, cut into thin strips
3 to 4 tbsp. olive oil, divided
1 medium onion, chopped
1 green bell pepper, chopped
1 10 oz. can enchilada sauce
1 15 oz. can Mexican-style stewed tomatoes
3 cups cooked white rice, hot

Combine the flour with the salt, black pepper, and cumin on a dinner plate. Dredge the strips of steak in the flour mixture.

Heat 2 tbsp. of the oil in a 12" skillet over medium-high heat. Add the meat and brown it on all sides. Remove the meat and set aside.

Add the remaining oil to the skillet. Turn the heat down to medium. Add the onion and green bell pepper. Sauté until tender.

Return the steak to the skillet. Add the enchilada sauce and the tomatoes. Bring to a boil, then reduce the heat to low and simmer, covered, for 30 minutes or until the steak is tender, stirring occasionally.

Serve over hot cooked white rice.

Serves 6

Black Bean Tortilla Bake

This is lasagna, San Antonio style.

1 lb. lean ground beef
1 small onion, chopped
1 19 oz. can enchilada sauce
1 15 oz. can black beans, drained and rinsed
1 8 oz. can whole kernel corn, drained
1 4.5 oz. can chopped green chiles
2 tbsp. chili powder
1 tsp. ground cumin
1 tsp. garlic salt
½ tsp. dried oregano
¼ tsp. black pepper
6 8" flour tortillas, divided
2 cups shredded cheddar cheese, divided
½ cup chopped cilantro

Brown the ground beef, along with the onion, in a 12" skillet over medium heat. Drain.

Add the enchilada sauce, beans, corn, and chiles. Stir to mix. Bring to a boil, then reduce the heat and simmer, uncovered, for 5 minutes.

Stir in the chili powder, cumin, garlic salt, oregano, and black pepper. Bring to a boil, then reduce the heat and simmer, uncovered, for 15 minutes.

While this is cooking, preheat the oven to 350 degrees. Lightly spray a 13x9" baking dish with cooking spray.

Place 3 tortillas on the bottom of the prepared baking dish, overlapping as needed. Spread half of the meat mixture and half of the cheese on top of the tortillas. Top with the remaining tortillas, meat mixture, and cheese. Sprinkle with cilantro. Bake, uncovered, for 30 minutes.

Serves 6

Corn Chip Casserole

My mom used to make this when I was a little kid. It was always one of my favorite dinners, and I still enjoy it now. It's a Hamburger Helper® kind of recipe—quick, easy, and delicious.

1 lb. lean ground beef
¼ cup chopped onion
1 10 oz. can enchilada sauce
1 8 oz. can tomato sauce
2⅓ cups Fritos®
1 cup shredded cheddar cheese
Sour cream
Shredded lettuce
Chopped tomatoes

Preheat the oven to 350 degrees.

Cook the ground beef and onion in a 12" skillet over medium-high heat. Drain.

Place the beef and onion, enchilada sauce, tomato sauce, and Fritos® in a 2-qt. casserole dish. Stir to mix, being careful not to break the chips.

Bake, covered, for 30 to 35 minutes.

Remove the cover and generously top with cheddar cheese. Return the casserole to the oven until the cheese melts.

Serve with sour cream, lettuce, and tomatoes on the side.

Serves 4

Variation: To make a **Chili Corn Chip Casserole,** add 1 15.5-oz. can red kidney beans.

Refried Tortilla Casserole

1 lb. lean ground beef
1 cup chopped onion
2 tbsp. chili powder
1 14.5 oz. can diced tomatoes, with juice
1 16 oz. can refried beans
1 10 oz. bag tortilla chips, crushed
1 cup shredded cheddar cheese
1 cup shredded Monterey jack cheese
Shredded lettuce
Chopped tomatoes
Avocado slices
Sour cream

Preheat the oven to 350 degrees. Lightly spray a 13x9" baking dish with nonstick cooking spray. Set aside.

Brown the ground beef with the onion in a 12" skillet over high heat. While the meat is cooking, stir in the chili powder. Drain.

Stir in the tomatoes. Heat to boiling, then reduce the heat and simmer for 5 minutes. Remove the pan from the heat.

Spread the refried beans in the bottom of the prepared baking dish. Sprinkle on half of the tortilla chips. Top with the beef mixture. Sprinkle with the remaining chips and top with both cheeses. Bake for 20 to 30 minutes or until the cheese is bubbling.

Top with shredded lettuce, chopped tomatoes, avocado slices, and sour cream.

Serves 4

South of the Border Casserole

1½ cups crushed nacho chips
1½ lb. lean ground beef
1 medium onion, chopped
1 garlic clove, chopped
1 10 oz. can enchilada sauce
1 cup sour cream
1 cup ricotta cheese
1 4.5 oz. can chopped green chiles
1 cup shredded Monterey jack cheese
1 cup shredded cheddar cheese
¼ cup sliced black olives

Preheat the oven to 350 degrees. Lightly spray a 13x9" baking dish with nonstick cooking spray.

Sprinkle the crushed chips evenly over the bottom of the prepared baking dish. Set aside.

Brown the ground beef in a 12" skillet over medium heat. Add the onion and garlic halfway through cooking. Drain.

Stir in the enchilada sauce. Heat through.

In a medium-size bowl, mix the sour cream, ricotta cheese, and chiles together.

Place the ground beef mixture over the crushed nachos. Spread the sour cream mixture over. Cover with cheese. Dot with olives. Bake for 40 to 45 minutes.

Serves 4

Salsa Beef Stew

2 to 3 tbsp. olive oil
2 lb. beef stew meat, cut in 1" pieces
1 large onion, coarsely chopped
1 green bell pepper, coarsely chopped
1 garlic clove, minced
2 cups beef broth
1 14.5 oz. can diced tomatoes, with juice
½ cup chunky salsa
Salt and black pepper to taste
3 tbsp. cornstarch blended with ¼ cup cold water
3 cups cooked white rice, hot

Heat the oil in a Dutch oven over medium-high heat. Add the beef and brown on all sides.

Add the onion, green bell pepper, and garlic. Cook until soft, about 5 minutes. Drain any remaining fat.

Add the broth, tomatoes, and salsa. Stir to mix. Season with salt and pepper. Bring to a boil, then reduce the heat and simmer, covered, for 2 hours, stirring occasionally.

Stir the cornstarch-water mixture slowly into the stew. Bring the heat up to medium high and cook until thickened, stirring occasionally. Serve over rice.

Serves 6

Stuffed Poblano Peppers

Chile Rellenos are poblano peppers stuffed with cheese. This recipe is reminiscent of stuffed green peppers—filled with the flavor of San Antonio.

- 1 8 oz. can tomato sauce
- 1 14.5 oz. can diced tomatoes, with juice
- 2 tbsp. chili powder
- 1 lb. lean ground beef, or ½ lb. lean ground beef and ½ lb. chorizo
- 1 15 oz. can black beans, drained, rinsed, and slightly mashed
- ½ cup instant rice, cooked
- ¼ cup chopped onion
- 1 jalapeño pepper, finely chopped
- 2 large poblano peppers, stemmed, seeded, and sliced in half
- ½ cup shredded cheddar cheese

Preheat the oven to 350 degrees. Lightly spray a 13x9" baking dish with cooking spray. Set aside.

In a medium-size bowl, combine the tomato sauce, diced tomatoes, and chili powder. Remove and reserve ¼ cup of this mixture.

In a large mixing bowl, combine the ground beef, beans, rice, onion, and jalapeño pepper.

Add the tomato mixture to the beef mixture and combine well. Stuff each half of the poblano pepper halves with the meat-tomato mixture.

Transfer the peppers to the prepared baking dish. Top with the remaining tomato mixture. Bake, uncovered, for 1 hour.

Sprinkle the cheese on top of the peppers. Return to the oven and bake for 5 more minutes or until the cheese melts.

Serves 4

Salsa-Style Meatloaf

This is not your average Monday night meatloaf. The crushed tortilla chips add a nice flavor and texture, which is much better than breadcrumbs.

2 lb. lean ground beef
1 large egg, lightly beaten
2 cups crushed tortilla chips
1½ cups salsa, divided
½ cup cheddar cheese
2 tbsp. chopped cilantro

Preheat the oven to 350 degrees. Lightly spray a 9" baking pan with cooking spray. Set aside.

In a large bowl, combine the ground beef, egg, tortilla chips, half of the salsa, the cheese, and cilantro. Mix well.

Transfer to the prepared baking dish. Shape into a loaf. Cover with the remaining salsa. Bake for 1 hour.

Serves 6

Tamale Meatloaf

Tamales are cooked meat, usually with peppers and spices, rolled in cornmeal, wrapped in cornhusks, then steamed or baked. This tamale meatloaf is a quick and easy replica.

1 lb. lean ground beef
1 large egg
1 medium onion, finely chopped
¾ cup salsa, divided
2 tbsp. chili powder
3 garlic cloves, minced
1 8.5 oz. package corn muffin mix
½ cup shredded cheddar cheese

Preheat the oven to 350 degrees.

In a large mixing bowl, combine the ground beef, egg, onion, ¼ cup salsa, chili powder, and garlic. Mix well.

Place the meat mixture in a 9" pie pan, shaping the mixture to fit the pan. Bake for 40 minutes.

While the meatloaf is cooking, prepare the batter for the muffin mix according to package directions.

Remove the meatloaf from the oven and spread the batter over the top of the meatloaf.

Return the meatloaf to the oven and bake for 20 more minutes or until the cornbread is done.

Remove the pan from the oven and top with cheddar cheese. Cover loosely with aluminum foil and let stand for 10 minutes.

Serve with the remaining salsa.

Serves 4

Tamale Pie

This recipe is filled with the flavors of San Antonio.

Filling:

4 tbsp. vegetable oil, divided
1 2 lb. boneless beef rump roast, cut into ½" cubes
1 large onion, chopped
2 jalapeño peppers, stemmed, seeded, and finely chopped
4 garlic cloves, finely chopped
2 tsp. unsweetened cocoa powder
1 tsp. cinnamon
1 tsp. salt
3 tbsp. chili powder
1 tsp. ground cumin
¼ tsp. ground allspice
¼ tsp. cayenne pepper
1 28 oz. can crushed tomatoes, with juice
1 10 oz. package frozen corn
1½ cups water
1 15.5 oz. can pinto beans, drained and rinsed
1 cup chopped pimiento-stuffed green olives
⅓ cup chopped fresh cilantro
Salt to taste

Topping:

1 cup all-purpose flour
1 cup yellow cornmeal
¾ cup grated cheddar cheese
1½ tbsp. sugar
2 tsp. baking powder
½ tsp. salt
½ tsp. ground cumin
¼ cup finely chopped fresh cilantro
1 jalapeño pepper, stemmed, seeded, and finely chopped
¾ cup milk
3 tbsp. unsalted butter, melted and cooled
1 large egg, lightly beaten

For Filling: Heat 3 tbsp. of oil in a 6-qt. Dutch oven over medium-high heat. Add the beef and brown on all sides. Remove the beef and set aside.

Add the remaining 1 tbsp. oil to the pan. Add the onion and jalapeños. Sauté until the onion is tender, about 4 minutes.

Reduce the heat to medium, then add the garlic, cocoa powder, cinnamon, salt, chili powder, cumin, allspice, and cayenne pepper. Cook, stirring, for 1 minute.

Return the beef to the pan, along with any accumulated juices. Stir in the tomatoes, corn, and water. Simmer, uncovered, stirring occasionally, until the meat is very tender, about 1½ hours.

Remove the pan from the heat and stir in the beans, olives, and cilantro. Add salt to taste. Transfer the mixture to a shallow 3-qt. baking dish.

When the beef mixture is almost done cooking, make the topping. Preheat the oven to 400 degrees.

For Topping: In a large mixing bowl, combine the flour, cornmeal, cheese, sugar, baking powder, salt, cumin, cilantro, and jalapeño.

In a small bowl, whisk together the milk, butter, and egg, then stir this into the flour mixture until just combined.

Drop the batter by large spoonfuls (about 8) over the beef mixture, spacing them evenly. Bake in the middle of the oven for 10 minutes.

Reduce the oven temperature to 350 degrees and bake for 30 minutes more or until the topping is cooked through.

Serves 6

Taco Pie

1 cup crushed tortilla chips
2 to 3 tbsp. butter, melted
1 lb. lean ground beef
1 1.25 oz. package taco seasoning, divided
2 tbsp. water
2 8 oz. packages cream cheese, softened
2 large eggs
2 cups shredded cheddar cheese
1 8 oz. container sour cream
2 tbsp. all-purpose flour
1 cup shredded lettuce
1 large tomato, chopped
1 4.25 oz. can sliced black olives, drained

Preheat the oven to 325 degrees. Lightly spray a 9" springform pan with nonstick cooking spray. Set aside.

In a medium-size bowl, combine the crushed tortilla chips with the melted butter. Press the mixture into the bottom of the pan. Bake for 10 minutes, then cool on a wire rack.

While the crust is baking, cook the ground beef in a 12" skillet over medium heat. Drain.

Reserve 1 tsp. of the taco seasoning. Stir the remaining taco seasoning and water into the beef. Cook over medium heat for 5 minutes or until the liquid evaporates.

With an electric mixer, beat the cream cheese at medium speed until fluffy.

Add the eggs and reserved taco seasoning. Beat until blended.

Add the cheddar cheese and mix well.

Spread the cream cheese mixture evenly over the cooled crust and up the sides of the pan.

Spoon the beef mixture over the cream cheese mixture.

In a small bowl, combine the sour cream and flour. Spread over the beef mixture. Bake for 25 minutes.

Cool the pan on a wire rack for 10 minutes, then run a knife around the edges and release the sides.

Sprinkle with lettuce, tomatoes, and olives.

Serves 4

Tejano Beef

This recipe is so named because it is like music in your mouth.

- 2 to 3 tbsp. olive oil
- 1½ lb. stew beef cubes
- 1 medium onion, chopped
- 1 green bell pepper, chopped
- 1 garlic clove, minced
- 1 14.5 oz. can diced tomatoes, with juice
- 1 4.5 oz. can diced green chiles
- 1 15.5 oz. can red kidney beans, drained and rinsed
- 1 cup frozen corn, thawed
- ½ cup sliced black olives
- ½ cup water
- 2 tbsp. chili powder
- ½ tsp. salt
- ¼ tsp. black pepper
- 1 cup grated cheddar cheese
- 3 cups cooked white rice, hot
- 1 cup corn chips

Heat the oil in a 12" skillet over medium-high heat. Add the beef and brown it on all sides.

Add the onion, green bell pepper, and garlic. Sauté until soft, about 5 minutes.

Add the tomatoes, chiles, beans, corn, olives, water, chili powder, salt, and black pepper. Stir to mix. Bring to a boil, then reduce the heat and simmer, covered, for 45 minutes, stirring occasionally.

Top with cheese. Cover and let cook for 3 minutes or until cheese melts.

Serve over rice. Sprinkle with the chips.

Serves 4

Chorizo Casserole

1 lb. chorizo sausage
3 tbsp. butter
1 medium onion, chopped
1 green bell pepper, chopped
2 cups long-grain rice
1 14.5 oz. can diced tomatoes, with juice
1 8 oz. can tomato sauce

Preheat the oven to 325 degrees. Lightly spray a 2-qt. casserole dish with nonstick cooking spray. Set aside.

Cook the chorizo in a 12" skillet over medium-high heat. Drain. Remove the meat from the pan and set aside.

Wipe out the skillet, then add the butter and melt it over medium heat. Add the onion and green bell pepper. Sauté until tender.

Add the rice. Cook, stirring for 5 minutes or until the rice is browned.

Add the chorizo, tomatoes, and tomato sauce. Stir to combine.

Place the mixture into the prepared casserole dish. Bake for 30 to 35 minutes or until the rice is done and the liquid is absorbed.

Serves 4

Tender Tex-Mex Pork

The pork will be very tender. If you have leftovers, which you probably won't because it's so good, shred the pork and use it in a bean and cheese quesadilla or wrap it in a soft flour tortilla with chopped lettuce, tomatoes, and cheese.

4 tbsp. olive oil
4 tbsp. chili powder
4 tbsp. red pepper flakes
1 tbsp. dried oregano
1 tsp. seasoned salt
1 tsp. ground cumin
2 garlic cloves, crushed
4 tbsp. chopped cilantro
1 tbsp. black pepper
½ cup chopped green onions
½ cup chopped red onions
1 4 lb. pork loin, cut into 2" cubes
1 14.5 oz. can chicken broth

In a large bowl, mix together all the ingredients except the pork and the broth.

Add the pork and coat evenly with the marinade. Cover and marinate in the refrigerator for 4 hours.

Preheat the oven to 350 degrees.

Place the pork in a roasting pan. Add the broth. Bake, covered, for 3½ to 4 hours, turning once.

Serves 8

Pork and Peppers

- 2 tbsp. olive oil
- 1 lb. lean pork, cut into ¼" pieces
- 2 green bell peppers, diced
- 1 jalapeño pepper, stemmed, seeded, and diced
- ½ cup chopped green onions
- 1 garlic clove, minced
- 1 tsp. cumin
- 1 tsp. chili powder
- Salt and black pepper to taste
- 3 cups cooked white rice, hot
- ½ cup shredded cheddar cheese
- ½ cup sour cream

Heat the oil in a 12" skillet over medium-high heat. Add the pork and stir for 5 minutes until browned. Add the green bell peppers and the jalapeño pepper. Sauté for 5 minutes or until softened. Add the green onions and garlic. Cook for 2 more minutes, stirring.

Add the cumin and chili powder. Reduce the heat to medium and cook, stirring occasionally, for 10 minutes or until the pork is cooked through and the vegetables are tender. Season to taste with salt and pepper.

Serve over rice. Top with cheese and sour cream.

Serves 4

Green Salsa Pork

Green salsa is made with tomatillos and is referred to as salsa verde.

1 16 oz. jar green salsa
1 8 oz. container sour cream
2 to 3 tbsp. olive oil
¾ lb. pork tenderloin, cubed
1 large onion, chopped
1 green bell pepper, chopped
3 garlic cloves, finely chopped
¾ cup shredded Monterey jack cheese, divided
4 8" flour tortillas

Preheat the oven to 400 degrees. Lightly spray a 9x9" square baking dish with nonstick cooking spray. Set aside.

In a medium-size bowl, mix the salsa and sour cream together. Set aside.

Heat the oil in a 12" skillet over medium-high heat. Add the pork, onion, green bell pepper, and garlic. Cook, stirring occasionally, until the pork is no longer pink and the vegetables are soft.

Reduce the heat to medium. Stir 2 cups of the salsa mixture into the pork mixture. Cook for 1 minute, stirring frequently. Remove the pan from the heat. Stir in ½ cup of the cheese.

Place 1 tortilla in the prepared baking dish. Top with one-third of the pork mixture. Repeat layers twice. Top with the remaining tortilla. Spoon the remaining salsa mixture over the top. Sprinkle with the remaining cheese. Cover loosely with aluminum foil and bake for 10 minutes or until heated through.

Serves 4

Mexican Pork Chops

This is one of my favorite recipes. There are two ways to make it and both are delicious. I prefer the stovetop method.

2 to 3 tbsp. olive oil
4 center loin pork chops, trimmed of fat
1 medium onion, chopped
1 green bell pepper, chopped
1 garlic clove, minced
¼ tsp. black pepper
1 tbsp. chili powder
¼ tsp. ground cumin
1½ cups water
1 15 oz. can Mexican stewed tomatoes, cut up
¾ cup long-grain white rice
1 cup shredded cheddar cheese

Preheat the oven to 350 degrees. Lightly spray a 13x9" baking dish with cooking spray. Set aside.

Heat the oil in a 12" skillet over medium-high heat. Add the pork chops and brown on both sides. Transfer to the prepared baking dish.

Add the onion, green bell pepper, and garlic to the skillet. Sauté in the pork drippings until tender. Season with the black pepper, chili powder, and cumin.

Add the water and tomatoes. Cover and simmer for 5 minutes to blend the flavors.

Sprinkle the rice over the pork chops. Pour the sauce over. Cover with aluminum foil and bake for 1 hour.

Uncover and sprinkle with cheese. Bake, uncovered, for 5 to 10 more minutes or until the cheese melts.

Stovetop / Variation: Return the pork chops to the sauce in the skillet. Prepare the rice separately. Cover and simmer for 45 minutes, stirring and turning occasionally. Serve over hot cooked rice. To make **Mexican Chicken Chops,** use 4 skinless, boneless chicken breasts instead of pork chops.

Serves 4

Pinto Pork

This delicious recipe takes all day to cook and makes a wonderful Saturday-night supper.

2 16 oz. packages dried pinto beans, rinsed
1 2 lb. boneless pork roast
4 tbsp. chili powder
3 tbsp. ground cumin
2 tsp. dried oregano
½ cup picante sauce
2 garlic cloves, minced
Salt and black pepper to taste
2 cups corn chips
1 medium onion, diced
1 large tomato, diced
1 cup grated cheddar cheese
1 avocado, coarsely chopped

Preheat the oven to 275 degrees.

Put the beans, pork roast, chili powder, cumin, oregano, picante sauce, and garlic in a large roasting pan. Cover with water. Bake for 10 to 12 hours, stirring every hour and turning the roast.

Remove the roast and shred the meat with two forks. Return the meat to the bean mixture. Mix together. Season to taste with salt and pepper.

Serve over corn chips. Top with onion, tomato, cheese, and chopped avocado.

Serves 6

Pork Tenderloin with Greens and Black-Eyed Peas

6 cups loosely packed chopped fresh kale
1 tbsp. paprika
2 tbsp. ground cumin
Salt and black pepper to taste
1 2 lb. pork tenderloin, cut into 12 slices
4 tbsp. olive oil, divided
1 medium onion, chopped
1 8 oz. container sliced mushrooms
1 15.5 oz. can black-eyed peas, rinsed and drained
2 cups Simply Salsa (page 217)

Bring 2 qt. of lightly salted water to a boil. Add the kale and cook for 4 minutes. Drain in a colander and rinse under cold water. Set aside.

Combine the paprika, cumin, salt, and pepper in a small bowl. Rub on all sides of the pork slices. Set aside.

Heat 2 tbsp. of the oil in a 12" skillet over medium heat. Add the onion and mushrooms. Sauté until the onion is tender and the mushrooms are browned.

Add the black-eyed peas, the cooked kale, and the salsa. Simmer for 5 minutes.

While this is cooking, heat the remaining 2 tbsp. of oil in a separate 12" skillet over medium-high heat. Add the pork slices and brown for 2 to 3 minutes on both sides or until cooked through.

Spoon some of the salsa mixture on individual plates. Place the pork slices on top and drizzle with additional salsa.

Serves 6

Chicken

Blackened Chicken

This chicken isn't burned. It blackens from the spice mixture.

6 tbsp. butter
1 garlic clove, pressed
4 tbsp. finely grated onion
1 tsp. cayenne pepper
2 tsp. paprika
1½ tsp. salt
1½ tsp. black pepper
¼ tsp. ground cumin
1 tsp. dried cilantro
6 skinless, boneless chicken breasts, sliced in half lengthwise

Melt the butter with the garlic in a 12" skillet over medium heat.

Combine the onion, cayenne pepper, paprika, salt, black pepper, cumin, and cilantro on a dinner plate.

Brush the chicken with half of the butter mixture on both sides, then coat with the spice mixture.

Drizzle the remaining butter mixture on each chicken breast. Place them in the skillet in a single layer, 2 or 3 at a time. Cook until the bottom begins to blacken, about 2 to 3 minutes, then turn over and cook the second side.

Serves 6

Cheddar Cilantro Chicken

This quick and easy dinner is delicious. Cilantro has a rather strong taste. If it's a bit too much for you, substitute parsley.

2 tsp. chili powder
¼ tsp. salt
¼ tsp. black pepper
4 skinless, boneless chicken breasts
2 to 3 tbsp. olive oil
1 15 oz. can black beans, drained and rinsed
1 cup frozen corn, thawed
½ cup salsa
Cooked white rice, hot
¼ cup shredded cheddar cheese
2 tbsp. freshly chopped cilantro

In a small bowl, combine the chili powder, salt, and pepper. Sprinkle over the chicken.

Heat the oil in a 12" skillet over medium-high heat. Add the chicken and brown on both sides.

Stir in the beans, corn, and salsa. Heat to boiling, then reduce the heat, cover, and simmer for 10 minutes or until the vegetables are tender and the chicken is cooked through.

Serve over rice. Sprinkle with cheese and cilantro.

Serves 4

Chicken Chipotle Mole

Mole is a sauce combining chocolate and chiles. In this recipe, chipotle chiles are used. Chipotle chiles in adobo sauce are available canned in the ethnic sections of grocery stores.

4 skinless, boneless chicken breasts, each cut into 3 pieces
2 tbsp. ground cumin
Salt and black pepper
1 tbsp. olive oil
1 large onion, thinly sliced
2 14.5 oz. cans chili-style chunky tomatoes in juice
1 cup chicken broth
2 tbsp. minced canned chipotle chiles
1 tbsp. adobo sauce
1 oz. unsweetened chocolate, chopped
Cooked white rice, hot

Coat the chicken on all sides with the cumin. Sprinkle with salt and black pepper.

Heat the oil in a 12" skillet over medium-high heat. Add the chicken and sauté until browned on all sides, about 5 minutes.

Add the onion and sauté until it begins to brown, about 3 minutes.

Add the tomatoes, broth, chipotle chiles, adobo sauce, and chocolate. Bring to a boil, then reduce the heat and simmer until the chicken is cooked through and the sauce thickens slightly, about 20 minutes.

Serve over hot rice.

Serves 4

Chicken Fiesta

A fiesta is a party, and the people of San Antonio are famous for their fiestas. You'll feel like celebrating when you enjoy this dish.

½ cup butter, melted
2 cups finely crushed Fritos®
2 tbsp. taco seasoning mix
4 skinless, boneless chicken breasts
2 tbsp. butter
1 small bunch green onions, chopped
1 tsp. dry chicken bouillon
2 cups heavy cream
1 cup grated Monterey jack cheese
1 cup grated sharp cheddar cheese

Preheat the oven to 350 degrees. Pour the melted butter into a 13x9" baking dish, spreading it evenly over the bottom. Set aside.

On a dinner plate, combine the crushed Fritos® and the taco mix. Dredge the chicken in the Fritos® mixture, coating it well on both sides. Place the chicken in the prepared baking dish.

Melt the 2 tbsp. butter in a 12" skillet over medium-high heat. Add the onions and sauté until soft.

Reduce the heat to low and stir in the chicken bouillon.

Add the heavy cream and both cheeses. Mix well. Stir gently until the cheese is melted.

Pour the sauce over the chicken. Bake, uncovered, for 55 minutes.

Serves 4

Doritos® Chicken

- 1 12 oz. package Doritos®, crushed
- 4 skinless, boneless chicken breasts, cooked and chopped
- 1 medium onion, chopped
- 1 red bell pepper, chopped
- 1 garlic clove, minced
- 1 15 oz. can Mexican stewed tomatoes
- ½ cup picante sauce
- Salt and black pepper to taste
- 1½ cups grated cheddar cheese

Preheat the oven to 375 degrees. Lightly spray a 13x9" baking dish with nonstick cooking spray.

Sprinkle the crushed chips evenly over the bottom of the prepared baking dish. Set aside.

In a large bowl, combine the cooked chicken, onion, red bell pepper, garlic, tomatoes, and picante sauce. Season with salt and black pepper to taste.

Pour the mixture over the crushed chips. Sprinkle with cheese. Bake for 40 minutes or until bubbly.

Serves 4

Jalapeño Chicken

2 tbsp. olive oil
4 skinless, boneless chicken breasts
1 medium onion, chopped
2 jalapeño peppers, stemmed, seeded, and chopped
8 garlic cloves, chopped
2 ribs celery, chopped
2 medium tomatoes, chopped
2 cups whole kernel corn
Juice and zest of 1 lime
2 tbsp. chili powder
Salt and black pepper to taste
¼ cup sliced black olives
3 cups cooked white rice, hot

Heat the oil in a 12" skillet over medium-high heat. Add the chicken and cook on both sides until brown. Remove and set aside.

Add the onion, jalapeños, garlic, and celery to the skillet. Sauté for 2 to 3 minutes or until vegetables have softened.

Add the tomatoes, corn, lime juice and zest, and the chili powder to the skillet. Stir to mix. Place the chicken on top. Reduce the heat, cover, and simmer for 10 minutes. Season to taste with salt and pepper.

Add the black olives and heat through.

Serve over hot rice.

Serves 4

Monterey Pepper Jack Chicken

Monterey pepper jack cheese, also known as jalapeño jack cheese, is sold in a block package. Just shred it for this recipe and you're good to go.

2 large eggs
2 tbsp. water
1 cup cornmeal
2 tbsp. Parmesan cheese
½ tsp. cumin
½ tsp. chili powder
½ tsp. cayenne pepper
4 skinless, boneless chicken breasts
2 cups salsa
1 cup shredded Monterey pepper jack cheese
3 cups cooked white rice, hot
1 8 oz. container sour cream

Preheat the oven to 425 degrees. Lightly spray a 13x9" baking dish with nonstick cooking spray. Set aside.

In a small bowl, whisk the eggs and water until frothy.

On a dinner plate, combine the cornmeal, Parmesan cheese, cumin, chili powder, and cayenne pepper.

Dip the chicken breasts in the egg, then dredge in the cornmeal mixture, coating evenly. Shake off the excess.

Place the chicken in the prepared baking dish and cook for 30 to 35 minutes or until the juices run clear when pierced with a sharp knife.

Remove the chicken from the oven and pour the salsa over. Sprinkle with the cheese. Return to the oven for 10 minutes or until the cheese melts.

Serve over rice with sour cream on the side.

Serves 4

Poblano Chicken

4 skinless, boneless chicken breasts
2 cups chicken broth
2 bay leaves
2 whole peppercorns
1 onion, coarsely chopped
3 ribs celery, coarsely chopped
2 carrots, coarsely chopped
2 tsp. ground cumin
1 8 oz. package cream cheese, softened
2 poblano peppers, roasted, peeled, and seeded
4 tbsp. butter
Salt and black pepper to taste

Place the chicken in a large saucepan. Add the chicken broth, bay leaves, peppercorns, onion, celery, carrots, and cumin. Bring to a boil, then reduce the heat and simmer for 20 minutes or until the chicken is cooked through. Drain, reserving the broth. Discard the bay leaves, peppercorns, onion, celery, and carrots. (These were used to season the chicken.)

Preheat the oven to 350 degrees. Lightly spray a 13x9" baking dish with cooking spray. Set aside.

Place the cream cheese, roasted poblano peppers, 1½ cups of the reserved chicken broth, and the butter in a blender. Blend until smooth and creamy. Season to taste with salt and black pepper.

Place the chicken in the prepared baking dish. Pour the poblano sauce over the chicken and bake, covered, for 20 minutes.

Serves 4

Chipotle Chicken

6 chipotle chiles
1 to 1½ cups chicken broth
3 tbsp. vegetable oil
3 medium onions, sliced
6 skinless, boneless chicken breasts
Salt and black pepper to taste
Cooked white rice, hot
Freshly chopped cilantro

Put the dried chiles in a bowl and pour in hot water to cover. Let stand for 30 minutes. Drain, reserving the soaking liquid in a measuring cup. Cut the stem off each chile, then slit them lengthwise and scrape out the seeds. Chop the chiles finely.

Put the chopped chiles into a blender. Add enough chicken broth to the soaking liquid to make 1⅔ cups. Pour into the blender and process until smooth.

Preheat the oven to 350 degrees. Lightly spray a 13x9" baking dish with nonstick cooking spray. Set aside.

Heat the oil in a 10" skillet over medium heat. Add the onions and cook for 5 minutes or until they are softened but not brown, stirring occasionally. Transfer the onions to the prepared baking dish, spreading them evenly over the bottom.

Place the chicken on top of the onions. Season with salt and pepper.

Pour the chipotle sauce over the chicken breasts, evenly coating each piece. Bake for 45 minutes or until the chicken is cooked through.

Serve over rice. Garnish with cilantro.

Serves 6

Chicken-Stuffed Poblanos

8 medium poblano peppers
½ tbsp. vegetable oil
1 large onion, finely chopped
¼ cup water
2 roma tomatoes, finely diced
2 cups chopped cooked chicken
1 tsp. salt
½ tsp. black pepper
6 oz. Monterey jack cheese, cut into ¼" cubes

Place the poblano peppers on a baking sheet and broil about 2 inches from the heat. Roast them, turning with tongs, until the skins are blistered but not blackened, about 4 to 6 minutes. Transfer the roasted peppers to a large plastic Ziploc bag and seal to allow the peppers to steam. Set aside.

Heat the vegetable oil in a 12" skillet over medium heat. Add the onion and cook, stirring, until the onion begins to turn golden, about 4 minutes.

Add the water and cook, stirring occasionally, until the water is evaporated and the onion is tender, about 5 minutes.

Add the tomatoes and cook, stirring, until softened, about 4 minutes. Remove the pan from the heat.

Stir in the cooked chicken, salt, and pepper.

Let cool completely, then stir in the cheese.

Preheat the oven to 350 degrees. Lightly spray a 13x9" baking dish with nonstick cooking spray. Set aside.

Rub the skins off the poblano peppers. Leaving the stem attached, carefully cut a slit lengthwise in each pepper. Remove the seeds.

Stuff the chicken mixture into the peppers through the slits, keeping the peppers intact. Place the stuffed peppers in the prepared baking dish. Cover tightly with aluminum foil and bake for 30 minutes.

Serves 8

Crunchy Chicken Olé

¼ cup butter, divided
1 medium red onion, finely chopped
1 green bell pepper, finely chopped
1 cup shredded Monterey jack cheese
½ cup shredded cheddar cheese
1 tbsp. chopped cilantro
6 skinless, boneless chicken breasts, pounded flat
2 tsp. ground cumin
1 tsp. chili powder
1 cup crushed Fritos®

Preheat the oven to 350 degrees. Lightly spray a 13x9" baking dish with cooking spray. Set aside.

Heat 2 tbsp. of the butter in a 12" skillet over medium heat. Add the onion and bell pepper. Sauté until tender.

Combine the Monterey jack and cheddar cheeses, the sautéed onion and bell pepper, and the cilantro in a medium-size bowl.

Place equal amounts of the cheese mixture on each chicken breast and roll up. Place seam side down in the prepared baking dish.

Melt the remaining butter in a small bowl in the microwave. Add the cumin and chili powder. Stir to mix. Pour the butter mixture over the chicken.

Cover with aluminum foil and bake for 45 minutes.

Remove from the oven, uncover, and top with the crushed chips. Return to the oven and bake for 5 more minutes.

Serves 6

Ranchero Chicken

This is San Antonio's version of Chicken Parmesan. While this recipe calls for homemade Ranchero Sauce, you can just as easily use a store-bought Ranchero Sauce, or you might want to experiment a bit, using jarred salsa or a tomatillo sauce.

2 to 3 tbsp. olive oil
4 skinless, boneless chicken breasts
1 onion, chopped
1 green bell pepper, chopped
2 cups Ranchero Sauce (page 219)
½ cup shredded cheddar cheese
2 green onions, sliced

Heat the oil in a 12" skillet over medium-high heat. Add the chicken and brown on both sides. Remove the chicken and set aside.

Reduce the heat to medium. Place the onion and bell pepper in the skillet, adding more oil if necessary. Sauté until tender.

Return the chicken to the skillet. Add the Ranchero Sauce. Bring to a boil, then reduce the heat, cover, and simmer for 20 minutes, stirring the sauce and turning the chicken occasionally.

Place on individual dinner plates. Sprinkle with cheddar cheese and top with the green onions.

Serves 4

San Antonio Chicken

This recipe starts from scratch, but you can substitute 1 6 oz. package Southwest-seasoned chicken breasts for the chopped chicken and taco seasoning, and 1 10-oz. bag chuckwagon corn or western vegetables for the onion, green bell pepper, corn, and pimientos.

- 2 skinless, boneless chicken breasts
- 1 1.25 oz. package taco seasoning
- 3 tbsp. water
- 2 to 3 tbsp. vegetable oil
- 1 medium onion, coarsely chopped
- 1 green bell pepper, coarsely chopped
- 1 cup frozen corn, thawed
- 1 2 oz. jar pimientos
- 1 15 oz. can black beans, drained and rinsed
- 3 cups cooked white rice, hot
- 1 cup picante sauce

Place the chicken in a saucepan and cover with water. Let simmer for 10 to 15 minutes or until the chicken is cooked through. Remove to a cutting board and coarsely chop the chicken.

In a medium-size bowl, toss the cooked, chopped chicken with the taco seasoning mix and water. Set aside.

Heat the oil in a 12" skillet over medium-high heat. Add the onion, green bell pepper, and corn. Sauté until tender.

Add the pimientos, black beans, chopped chicken, rice, and picante sauce. Stir to mix and heat through.

Serves 4

Serrano-Stuffed Chicken

Feel free to get creative with this basic recipe. Add pimientos, sun-dried tomatoes, chopped black olives, or diced green onions into the stuffing.

3 serrano peppers, roasted, peeled, stemmed, seeded, and cut in half
½ 8 oz. brick Monterey Jack cheese, cut into 6 strips
6 skinless, boneless chicken breasts, pounded flat
¼ cup chicken broth
¼ tsp. paprika

Preheat the oven to 350 degrees. Lightly spray a 13x9" baking dish with cooking spray. Set aside.

Stuff the serrano peppers with the cheese strips.

Place each stuffed serrano on a chicken breast. Roll up and secure with a wooden toothpick if necessary.

Place seam side down in the prepared baking dish. Pour the chicken broth over. Bake, uncovered, for 20 minutes, basting once or twice.

Remove the toothpicks and sprinkle with paprika before serving.

Serves 6

Chicken and Black Bean Casserole

- 2 tbsp. butter
- 1 medium red onion, thinly sliced
- 5 garlic cloves, minced
- 2 cups shredded cooked chicken
- 1 15 oz. can black beans, drained and rinsed
- 1 cup chicken broth
- 1 8 oz. jar salsa
- 10 6" corn tortillas, cut into 1" strips
- 1 cup shredded Monterey jack cheese

Preheat the oven to 450 degrees. Lightly spray a 13x9" baking dish with nonstick cooking spray. Set aside.

Melt the butter in a 12" skillet over medium-high heat. Add the onion and sauté for 5 minutes or until lightly browned. Add the garlic and sauté for 1 minute.

Add the cooked chicken and heat through. Transfer the mixture to a medium-size bowl. Stir in the beans. Set aside.

Add the broth and salsa to the skillet and bring to a boil. Reduce the heat and simmer for 5 minutes, stirring occasionally.

Place half of the tortilla strips in the bottom of the prepared baking dish. Layer half of the chicken mixture over the tortillas. Top with the remaining tortillas and chicken mixture. Pour the broth mixture evenly over the chicken mixture. Sprinkle with cheese. Bake for 10 minutes or until the cheese is melted and lightly browned.

Serves 4

Chicken and Corn Tortilla Casserole

1½ cups chicken broth
1 cup milk
½ cup flour
1 8 oz. container sour cream
1 14.5 oz. can diced tomatoes
1 4.5 oz. can chopped green chiles
¼ cup fresh chopped cilantro
1 tbsp. chili powder
1 tsp. dried oregano
½ tsp. ground cumin
Salt and black pepper to taste
1½ tsp. olive oil
1 large onion, chopped
1 green bell pepper, diced
2 garlic cloves, minced
2 cups cooked chicken, diced
10 corn tortillas, cut in quarters
½ cup shredded cheddar cheese

Preheat the oven to 375 degrees.

Bring the chicken broth to a simmer in a medium saucepan.

In a small bowl, whisk together the milk and flour to make a paste.

Add the paste to the broth and cook, whisking constantly, until the broth is thickened and smooth, about 3 minutes.

Remove the pan from the heat and stir in the sour cream, tomatoes, chiles, cilantro, chili powder, oregano, and cumin. Season to taste with salt and pepper. Set aside.

Heat the oil in a 12" skillet over medium-high heat. Add the onion, green bell pepper, and garlic. Cook, stirring occasionally, until tender crisp, about 3 minutes.

Line the bottom of a shallow 3-qt. baking dish with half of the tortillas. Top with half of the chicken and half of the onion mixture. Spoon half of the sauce evenly over the top. Repeat layers with the remaining tortillas, chicken, onion mixture, and sauce. Sprinkle the top with cheese and bake for 25 to 30 minutes.

Serves 4

Chicken Chile Casserole

This casserole has it all in one dish—chicken, rice, and beans.

4 skinless, boneless chicken breasts, cut into strips
1 tbsp. chili powder
Salt and black pepper to taste
1 cup quick-cooking brown rice
1 15 oz. can black beans, drained and rinsed
1 4.5 oz. can diced green chiles
⅛ tsp. cumin
⅛ tsp. cayenne pepper
⅛ tsp. garlic powder
¼ tsp. onion powder
¼ tsp. dried oregano
¼ cup grated cheddar cheese

Preheat the oven to 350 degrees. Lightly spray a 13x9" baking dish with nonstick cooking spray.

Arrange the chicken in the baking dish. Sprinkle with chili powder, salt, and pepper. Bake for 20 minutes.

Cook the rice according to the package directions, except substitute chicken broth for water.

When the rice is done, mix in the black beans, chiles, cumin, cayenne pepper, garlic powder, onion powder, and oregano.

Pour the drippings from the cooked chicken into the rice mixture. Stir well, then spread the rice mixture over the chicken.

Top with the cheese. Return to the oven for 5 minutes to melt the cheese.

Serves 4

Chicken Chilaquiles Casserole

Chilaquiles are day-old tortillas, which can be used in a variety of ways. This recipe is made with corn tortillas, chicken, salsa, tomatillos, and topped with Mexican Blend cheese.

2 cups chicken broth
4 skinless, boneless chicken breasts
3 cups salsa
½ cup heavy cream
1 tsp. salt
½ tsp. black pepper
1 large onion, thinly sliced
12 tomatillos, husked, cored, and thinly sliced
2½ cups grated Mexican Blend cheese
12 6" corn tortillas, warmed

Bring the chicken broth to a boil in a large saucepan. Place the chicken in the broth and reduce the heat to low. Cover and cook until tender, about 15 minutes. Set aside to cool in the broth. When cool, shred the chicken with two forks.

In a large mixing bowl, combine the salsa, cream, salt, pepper, onion, tomatillos, and shredded chicken.

Preheat the oven to 350 degrees. Lightly spray a 4-qt. casserole dish with nonstick cooking spray.

Spread a thin layer of cheese over the bottom of the prepared baking dish.

Push the solids in the bowl of chicken and salsa to the side so that the liquid forms in a pool on one side. Dip all the warmed tortillas, one at a time, in the pool of liquid to moisten.

Layer one-third of the moist tortillas over the cheese. Top with half of the chicken mixture with its sauce. Sprinkle half of the remaining cheese over the chicken. Repeat the layers, ending with a layer of tortillas on the top. Cover tightly with aluminum foil.

Bake for 30 minutes or until the edges are slightly brown. Let sit for 10 minutes before slicing.

Serves 4

Chorizo Chicken Casserole

Roasting the tomatoes and toasting the rice adds a nice dimension to this dish.

4 large tomatoes
Olive oil
Salt and black pepper to taste
4 skinless, boneless chicken breasts
½ cup all-purpose flour, mixed with salt and black pepper
4 to 5 tbsp. olive oil
1 large onion, coarsely chopped
1 garlic clove, coarsely chopped
1 cup long-grain white rice
2 cups chicken broth
½ cup diced pimiento
½ lb. cooked chorizo sausage
2 cups frozen black-eyed peas, thawed
½ cup sliced black olives
¼ cup chopped fresh cilantro

To roast the tomatoes, preheat the oven to 300 degrees. Lightly rub the tomatoes with olive oil, then sprinkle with salt and black pepper. Place on a baking sheet and roast in the oven for 15 to 20 minutes or until the tomatoes are softened. Place in a bowl, remove the skins, coarsely chop, and set aside.

Dredge the chicken breasts in the flour mixture.

Heat the oil in a 12" skillet over medium-high heat. Add the chicken and brown on both sides. Remove and set aside.

Add the onion and garlic to the skillet, adding more oil if necessary. Sauté until tender.

Add the rice and stir to coat with the oil. Let cook for 3 to 4 minutes, stirring occasionally, to toast the rice.

Add the roasted tomatoes, with their juices, the chicken broth, pimiento, and cooked chorizo to the skillet. Stir to mix.

Place the chicken breasts on top. Cover, reduce the heat to low, and simmer for 20 minutes, stirring occasionally.

Stir in the black-eyed peas. Cover and cook for 10 more minutes.

Add the olives. Heat through, then sprinkle with cilantro.

Serves 4

Tortilla Chip Chicken Casserole

1 10 oz. can chicken broth
4 skinless, boneless chicken breasts
1 28 oz. can diced tomatoes
1 medium onion, coarsely chopped
2 garlic cloves, peeled
2 canned chipotle chiles
¼ cup chopped fresh cilantro
Salt and black pepper to taste
15 5" corn tostadas, or 8 cups corn tortilla chips, broken into 2" pieces
1½ cups shredded Monterey jack cheese
1 8 oz. container sour cream

Pour the chicken broth into a saucepan. Add the chicken and bring to a simmer. Cook for 15 to 20 minutes or until the chicken is cooked through. Remove the chicken and let cool. Reserve the chicken broth. When cool, shred the chicken with two forks. Set aside.

Preheat the oven to 425 degrees. Lightly spray a 13x9" baking dish with nonstick cooking spray. Set aside.

Put the tomatoes, onion, garlic, and chiles in a blender. Purée until smooth.

Pour the tomato mixture into a medium saucepan over medium heat. Let simmer until slightly thickened, about 5 to 7 minutes.

Add the shredded chicken, reserved broth, and cilantro. Heat through. Season to taste with salt and pepper.

Place half of the chips in the prepared baking dish. Top with half of the tomato purée and chicken mixture and half of the cheese. Repeat with the second layer. Bake for 12 to 15 minutes or until bubbly and the cheese begins to brown.

Serve with sour cream on the side.

Serves 4

Chicken Fajitas

Fajitas are popular everywhere not just in San Antonio. Serve with a side of rice and beans, and imagine yourself eating them at an outdoor cafe on the River Walk. Instead of grilling the chicken and bell peppers, as is traditionally done, stir-fry them in a skillet.

3 skinless, boneless chicken breasts, cut into strips
Finely grated zest and juice of 2 limes
2 tbsp. sugar
2 tsp. dried oregano
½ tsp. cayenne pepper
1 tsp. ground cinnamon
3 tbsp. vegetable oil
2 medium onions, thinly sliced
1 red bell pepper, cut into strips
1 yellow bell pepper, cut into strips
1 green bell pepper, cut into strips
12 8" flour tortillas, warmed
1 cup guacamole
1 cup salsa
1 cup sour cream

Place the chicken strips into a large bowl. Add the lime zest and juice, sugar, oregano, cayenne pepper, and cinnamon. Mix thoroughly. Set aside to marinate for 30 minutes.

Heat the oil in a 12" skillet over medium-high heat. Stir-fry the marinated chicken for 5 to 6 minutes, then add the onions and bell peppers. Cook for 3 to 4 more minutes or until the chicken strips are cooked through and the vegetables are soft.

Spoon the chicken mixture into a serving bowl. Serve with warm tortillas, guacamole, salsa, and sour cream on the side.

Serves 6

Cumin Chicken Fajitas

There are many ways to make fajitas. Experiment with various spices to find the recipe you like best.

3 tbsp. vegetable oil
4 skinless, boneless chicken breasts, cut into strips
1 large onion, sliced
1 red bell pepper, thinly sliced
1 green bell pepper, thinly sliced
¼ tsp. ground cumin
¼ tsp. paprika
¼ tsp. cayenne pepper
¼ tsp. garlic powder
¼ tsp. dried oregano
¼ tsp. dried thyme
½ cup chicken broth
12 7" flour tortillas, warmed
1 tomato, chopped
1 avocado, peeled, pitted, and chopped
1 cup salsa

Heat the oil in a 12" skillet over medium-high heat. Add the chicken strips and brown on all sides. Remove and set aside.

Add the onion and bell peppers to the skillet, adding more oil if necessary. Sauté until almost tender, about 10 minutes.

Add the cumin, paprika, cayenne pepper, garlic powder, oregano, and thyme. Cook for 1 minute.

Mix in the broth and bring to a boil.

Add the chicken and stir until cooked through and the liquid has evaporated, about 5 minutes. (The broth will make the chicken strips nice and juicy.)

Spoon the chicken mixture into warmed tortillas. Top with chopped tomato and avocado. Fold the tortillas in half. Serve the salsa on the side.

Serves 6

Quickie Chicken Fajitas

5 tbsp. vegetable oil, divided
¼ cup fresh lime juice
3 garlic cloves, minced
½ tsp. salt
¼ tsp. black pepper
½ tsp. fajita seasoning*
4 skinless, boneless chicken breasts, pounded thin
1 large red onion, sliced
1 large red bell pepper, sliced
1 large green bell pepper, sliced
12 6" flour tortillas, warmed
1 cup Pico de Gallo (page 24)
1 8 oz. container sour cream

In a large mixing bowl, whisk together 2 tbsp. vegetable oil, lime juice, garlic, salt, black pepper, and fajita seasoning. Add the chicken and turn to coat. Cover and refrigerate for 30 minutes to 1 hour.

Heat 2 tbsp. oil in a 12" skillet over medium-high heat. Add the onion and bell peppers. Sauté for 3 to 4 minutes or until the onion is soft and the bell peppers are tender crisp. Remove to a bowl and cover to keep warm.

Put the remaining 1 tbsp. of oil into the skillet and heat over medium-high heat.

Remove the chicken from the marinade. Discard marinade.

Add the chicken to the skillet and sauté until cooked through, about 3 minutes per side. Remove the chicken to a cutting board and cut into 1" wide strips.

Arrange the chicken with the bell peppers and onion on a serving platter. Serve with warmed tortillas, Pico de Gallo, and sour cream.

Serves 6

*Fajita seasoning is sold in the spice section of grocery stores. In addition to seasoning chicken and beef for fajitas, it adds a wonderful flavor and kick when shaken into mashed potatoes and sprinkled on top of vegetables.

Seafood

Ceviche Salmon

Ceviche is a dish of small pieces of seafood marinated in citrus juice. This recipe uses salmon, which is cooked in the acid from the lime juice.

1 lb. salmon fillet, cut into strips
1 small onion, finely chopped
1 jalapeño pepper, stemmed, seeded, and finely chopped
Juice of 3 limes
1 tbsp. olive oil
1 tbsp. chopped fresh cilantro, plus more for garnish
½ tbsp. chives or dill
Salt and black pepper to taste
1 to 2 cups shredded lettuce
2 tomatoes, peeled and diced

In a medium-size, nonmetallic bowl, combine the fish, onion, jalapeño, lime juice, olive oil, cilantro, and chives. Cover and marinate in the refrigerator for 8 hours, stirring occasionally so the fish is well coated in the marinade.

When ready to serve, remove from the refrigerator and season to taste with salt and black pepper.

To serve, arrange the salmon atop a bed of lettuce on a serving platter. Top with the tomatoes and sprinkle with freshly chopped cilantro.

Serves 4

Chipotle Salmon

The sauce from canned chipotle chiles adds a nice, smoky flavor to the salmon.

4 garlic cloves, chopped
2 tbsp. olive oil
⅛ tsp. ground allspice
⅛ tsp. ground cinnamon
Juice of 2 limes
2 tsp. sauce from canned chipotle chiles
¼ tsp. ground cumin
Salt and black pepper to taste
4 salmon steaks
Lime slices, for garnish

In a medium-size bowl, combine the garlic, olive oil, allspice, cinnamon, lime juice, chipotle sauce, cumin, salt, and black pepper.

Coat the salmon with the marinade, then cover with plastic wrap and let marinate in the refrigerator for 1 hour.

Preheat the broiler. Transfer the salmon to a broiler pan and cook for 3 to 4 minutes on each side or until cooked through.

To serve, garnish with lime slices.

Serves 4

Tequila Salmon

Who says tequila has to be mixed into a drink?

3 tbsp. olive oil, divided
1 small onion, finely chopped
⅔ cup water
Grated zest and juice of 1 lime
½ cup light cream
3 jalapeño peppers, roasted, peeled, seeded, and chopped
Salt and black pepper to taste
3 tbsp. tequila
4 salmon fillets
1 avocado, sliced

Heat 1 tbsp. of the oil in a 12" skillet over medium-high heat. Add the onion and sauté until soft.

Add the water, lime zest, and lime juice. Cook for 10 minutes or until the sauce begins to reduce.

Reduce the heat to low. Stir in the cream. Add the jalapeño peppers. Simmer, stirring constantly for 2 to 3 minutes. Season to taste with salt and black pepper.

Add the tequila and stir to mix. Turn off the heat and cover to keep warm.

Brush the top of the salmon fillets with 1 tbsp. of the olive oil.

Heat a separate 12" skillet over high heat. Add the salmon, oiled side down. Cook for 2 to 3 minutes or until the underside is golden, then brush the top with the remaining 1 tbsp. of the olive oil. Turn each fillet over and cook the other side until the fish flakes easily when tested with a fork.

Spoon the tequila sauce on four dinner plates. Place the fish on top of the sauce, then top with avocado slices.

Serves 4

Salmon with Chipotle Sauce

This zesty, juicy salmon entrée comes with its own version of tartar sauce.

4 salmon fillets
1 canned chipotle pepper in adobo sauce, plus 1 tsp. of the sauce
½ cup mayonnaise
Grated zest and juice of 1 orange

Lightly spray a 12" skillet with olive-oil-flavored cooking spray. Heat over medium heat. Add the salmon and cook for 2½ minutes on each side.

While the salmon is cooking, mince the chipotle pepper and place in a small bowl. Stir in the adobo sauce, mayonnaise, and orange zest and juice.

Serve the chipotle sauce on the side with the salmon.

Serves 4

Chippy Cod

1½ lb. cod fillets
1 cup salsa
1 cup shredded cheddar cheese
½ cup crushed corn chips
¼ cup sour cream
1 avocado, sliced
¼ cup sliced black olives

Preheat the oven to 400 degrees. Lightly spray a 13x9" baking dish with nonstick cooking spray.

Place the fish fillets in the prepared baking dish. Cover each fillet with salsa and cheddar cheese. Top with crushed corn chips. Bake, uncovered, for 15 minutes or until the fish flakes easily with a fork.

To serve, top each fillet with sour cream, avocado slices, and black olives.

Serves 6

Corpus Christi Crab Cakes

Corpus Christi is about a two hour's drive from San Antonio and is a great beach get away.

2 medium eggs
2 tbsp. finely chopped green onion
1 2 oz. jar pimientos, drained
2 tbsp. mayonnaise
1 tbsp. chopped parsley
2 tsp. Dijon mustard
½ tsp. dried thyme
½ tsp. Worcestershire sauce
½ cup crushed seasoned croutons, divided
1 tbsp. chili powder
2 tbsp. grated Parmesan cheese
1 6 oz. package frozen crabmeat, thawed, or 1 6 oz. can crabmeat, drained, flaked, and cartilage removed
½ tsp. cayenne pepper
¼ cup cornmeal
2 tbsp. olive oil

In a medium-size mixing bowl, combine the eggs, green onion, pimientos, mayonnaise, parsley, mustard, thyme, Worcestershire sauce, ¼ cup crushed croutons, chili powder, and Parmesan cheese. Add the crab and mix well. Shape into patties about ¾" thick.

In another bowl, combine the remaining croutons and cayenne pepper with the cornmeal. Coat each side of the crab cakes with this mixture. (If they fall apart, just pat them back together and sprinkle with the cornmeal mixture.)

Heat the oil in a 12" nonstick skillet over medium heat. Add the crab cakes and cook for 3 minutes on each side or until they are golden and heated through. Add more oil if necessary.

Serves 4

Hacienda Halibut

1 16 oz. package frozen halibut fillets
2 tbsp. butter, melted
1 jalapeño pepper, stemmed, seeded, and sliced
1 8 oz. jar thick and chunky salsa
1 2.5 oz. can sliced black olives

Preheat the oven to 350 degrees.

Place the frozen halibut in a 13x9" baking dish. Cover with aluminum foil and bake for 25 minutes.

Pour the melted butter over each fillet. Top with the jalapeño slices, then salsa. Sprinkle the black olives over the salsa. Return to the oven and continue to bake, uncovered, for 15 more minutes.

Serves 4

Orange Roughy, Southwestern Style

4 orange roughy fillets
½ tsp. cumin
½ tsp. oregano
1 cup salsa

Lightly spray each fillet with nonstick cooking spray. Sprinkle each side of each fillet with cumin and oregano.

Heat a 12" skillet over medium heat. Add the fillets and cook for 3 minutes on the first side. Flip each fillet and top the cooked side with salsa.

Reduce the heat to medium low. Simmer for 6 minutes.

Serves 4

Cilantro Shrimp

Mary Trevino, owner of El Mirador restaurant (www.elmiradorrestaurant.com), is ninety-seven years old and still works at the restaurant six days a week. They've been serving authentic Mexican dishes, like this one, made from scratch with fresh ingredients since 1967.

Sauce:
2 tsp. olive oil
20 large shrimp, cleaned and deveined
2 garlic cloves, minced
2 tbsp. white wine
2 tsp. chopped cilantro, plus more for garnish
1½ tbsp. pesto*
½ cup heavy cream
4 tbsp. butter, cut into small pieces
Salt and black pepper to taste
3 cups cooked white rice, hot

Pesto:
3 bunches cilantro
½ cup pepitas (hulled pumpkin seeds)
½ cup Parmesan cheese
½ to 1 cup olive oil

Heat 2 tsp. oil in a 12" skillet over medium-high heat. Add the shrimp and garlic and sauté for 2 to 3 minutes. Remove the shrimp and set aside.

Add the wine to the skillet and stir to scrape up any drippings.

Add the cilantro, pesto, heavy cream, and butter to the skillet. Reduce the heat to low and cook just until the butter melts and the mixture is thickened. Be careful not to overcook or the sauce will separate.

Return the shrimp to the skillet. Season to taste with salt and black pepper.

Serve over hot rice. Garnish with cilantro.

Serves 4

***For Pesto:** Mix the cilantro, pepitas, and Parmesan cheese in a food processor. Blend until finely chopped. With the machine running, add the oil to incorporate the ingredients. (Use the remaining pesto to season the rice or use as a topping for tacos or tostadas.)

Serrano Shrimp

2 large tomatoes
2 to 3 tbsp. butter
1 tbsp. olive oil
1 red onion, chopped
2 garlic cloves, chopped
1 green bell pepper, chopped
2 serrano peppers, seeded and chopped
Salt and black pepper to taste
1 lb. shrimp, peeled and deveined
2 cups cooked white rice, hot

Preheat the broiler.

Place the tomatoes in a shallow baking pan about 5 inches from the heat. Broil for 5 minutes, then turn over and broil on the other side for 3 minutes. Remove and let cool, then core, peel, and coarsely chop the tomatoes, reserving the juices.

Melt the butter with the oil in a 12" skillet over medium heat. Add the onion, garlic, green bell pepper, and serrano peppers. Sauté until soft.

Add the tomatoes with their juices. Season with salt and black pepper to taste. Cover, reduce the heat, and simmer for 15 minutes.

Add the shrimp and stir. Cover and simmer for 5 more minutes.

Serve over rice.

Serves 4

Shrimp with Chipotle Remoulade Sauce

Jim Peyton, author of Jim Peyton's New Cooking from Old Mexico, *shares one of his all-time favorite recipes. It is a dish that delivers a great deal more than goes into it. This recipe is adapted from one by Emeril Lagasse whose cooking is similar to that of many of the practitioners of Mexico's upscale* la nueva cocina Mexicana, *a fusion of traditional ingredients with modern combinations. It adds a much-needed change to the traditional shrimp cocktail.*

Chipotle Remoulade:

2 tbsp. fresh lime juice
3 tbsp. olive oil
3 tbsp. canola oil
¼ cup chopped onion
¼ cup chopped celery
1 tbsp. chopped garlic
1 or 2 canned chipotle chiles, seeded and chopped, or to taste
1½ tbsp. Dijon mustard
1½ tbsp. American yellow mustard
1½ tbsp. ketchup
⅓ cup loosely packed, chopped cilantro
½ tsp. salt
¼ tsp. black pepper

Shrimp and Garnish:

1 lb. large shrimp (approx. 20)
1 large cucumber
1 small jicama
1 to 4 carved radishes

For Chipotle Remoulade: Place all the ingredients in a food processor fitted with a steel blade and process for 1 minute.

For Shrimp and Garnish: Clean and devein the shrimp, leaving the tails intact. Heat a large pot of water to boiling over high heat. Place the shrimp in the boiling water and cook them, checking them frequently by cutting into them with a small sharp knife, until they are just cooked through. Immediately immerse the shrimp in ice water, then refrigerate until thoroughly chilled.

Slice the cucumber and jicama into thin pieces and place them on a large serving platter to form a bed for the shrimp. When chilled, dry and place the shrimp on the platter and decorate with the carved radishes. Serve with remoulade.

Serves 6

Breads and Tortillas

Basic Cornbread

Cornbread goes great with chili as well as with soups and stews.

1 cup yellow cornmeal
1½ cups all-purpose flour
¾ cup sugar
4 tsp. baking powder
1 tsp. salt
1 cup milk
2 large eggs
¼ cup vegetable oil

Preheat the oven to 425 degrees. Lightly butter a 13x9" baking dish. Set aside.

In a large bowl, mix all the ingredients together just until moistened.

Pour the batter into the prepared baking dish. Let the batter sit for 5 minutes. (Letting the batter sit will create a nice top crust.)

Bake for 20 to 25 minutes.

Let cool slightly, then cut into squares. Serve warm.

Serves 8

Cheesy Chiles Cornbread

There's nothing better than cornbread to go with your chili. This version is especially spicy due to the addition of green chiles.

1 cup yellow cornmeal
3 tsp. baking powder
1 cup shredded cheddar cheese
2 medium eggs
½ cup vegetable oil
½ cup sour cream
1 tbsp. diced pimiento
1 4.5 oz. can diced green chiles
1 8.25 oz. can cream-style corn, drained

Preheat the oven to 400 degrees. Butter and lightly flour a 9" square baking dish. Set aside.

In a large bowl, mix together the cornmeal, baking powder, and cheese just until combined.

In a separate, medium bowl, whisk together the eggs, oil, sour cream, pimiento, chiles, and corn until well combined.

Add this to the cornmeal mixture. Stir just until moistened. Let sit for 5 minutes. (This will form a nice top crust.)

Pour the batter into the prepared baking dish. Bake for 50 to 60 minutes. Let cool on a wire rack for 10 minutes before removing from the pan.

Serves 4

Jalapeño Cornbread

4 strips bacon, diced
1 cup all-purpose flour
1 cup yellow cornmeal
¼ cup sugar
4 tsp. baking powder
2 medium eggs
4 tbsp. milk
1 cup sour cream
¼ cup butter, melted
1 8.25 oz. can cream-style corn, drained
3 jalapeño peppers, stemmed, seeded, and finely diced

Preheat the oven to 350 degrees. Lightly butter and flour a 9" square baking dish. Set aside.

Cook the bacon in a 10" skillet over medium heat just until the fat is rendered and the bacon is soft. Drain on paper towels and set aside.

Combine the flour, cornmeal, sugar, and baking powder in a large mixing bowl.

In a separate, medium-size mixing bowl, whisk the eggs with the milk. Add the sour cream, melted butter, creamed corn, and jalapeños.

Add the egg mixture to the flour mixture. Blend thoroughly.

Pour the batter into the prepared pan. Sprinkle the bacon evenly over the batter. Bake for 45 minutes. Let cool on a wire rack for 10 minutes before removing from the pan.

Serves 4

Southwest Cornbread

Instead of starting from scratch, this innovative recipe offers you both convenience and versatility.

½ cup Miracle Whip salad dressing
1 4.5 oz. can chopped green chiles
2 large eggs, lightly beaten
½ tsp. ground cayenne pepper
2 8.5 oz. packages corn muffin mix
1 11 oz. can whole kernel corn, drained
1 small red bell pepper, chopped

Preheat the oven to 400 degrees. Lightly butter a 13x9" baking dish. Set aside.

In a large bowl, mix salad dressing, chiles, eggs, and cayenne pepper.

Add the corn muffin mix, corn, and red bell pepper. Mix just until moistened.

Pour the batter into the prepared baking dish. Bake for 25 to 30 minutes or until golden.

Serves 8

Corn Tortillas

Masa is a dough made from ground hominy used to make tortillas and tamales. Masa harina is the dried and powered form. You can find it in the baking or ethnic section of large supermarkets.

2 cups masa harina de maiz (corn)
1½ cups warm water

Combine the masa harina de maiz and water in a medium-size mixing bowl. Mix with your hands into a soft dough.

Turn the dough out onto a floured surface and knead it until smooth.

Using 3 tbsp. as a measure, form the dough into balls. Keep them covered with a damp cloth.

Cut a large Ziploc plastic bag open down both of the sides.

Place the balls, one at a time, on one side of the plastic, cover with the other side, and use a rolling pin to press out the tortilla.

Cook the tortillas, one at a time, on a hot comal or skillet until they are lightly browned on each side. (A comal is a round, low-sided skillet similar to a griddle, which is used to cook tortillas.)

Yields 18

Flour Tortillas

Fresh, homemade flour tortillas are so much better than packaged tortillas. Make them once and you'll never buy packaged tortillas again. Many Mexican restaurants make their tortillas fresh in-house. They're served warm in a tortilla warmer.

3 cups all-purpose flour
3 tsp. baking powder
1 tsp. salt
4 tbsp. vegetable oil
1 cup warm water

Sift the flour, baking powder, and salt into a large mixing bowl. Add the vegetable oil and water. Mix with your fingers until well blended.

Turn the mixture out onto a floured surface and knead for 3 to 5 minutes or until the dough is soft and no longer sticky. Cover with a damp kitchen towel and set aside for 20 to 30 minutes.

Divide the dough into 18 balls about 1½ inches in diameter. Keep them covered with a damp cloth.

Roll out each ball on a floured surface with a rolling pin into a circle about 6" in diameter and ⅛" thick.

Cook the tortillas, one at a time, on a hot comal or skillet until they are lightly browned on each side.

Yields 18

Armadillo Biscuits

This recipe is from a San Antonio firefighter. These biscuits are hot and fiery and look like armadillos.

1 16 oz. bag shredded Monterey jack cheese
1 16 oz. bag shredded cheddar cheese
1½ cups buttermilk biscuit mix
1 lb. chorizo sausage, cooked
1 26 oz. can jalapeño peppers
2 large eggs
2 tbsp. water
1 1.25 oz. packet Shake 'n Bake Original Pork seasoned coating mix

Preheat the oven to 350 degrees. Lightly spray a 13x9" baking dish with cooking spray. Set aside.

Combine both cheeses in a large bowl.

In a separate large bowl, combine the biscuit mix, cooked chorizo, and half of the mixed cheeses. Mix well and shape into patties large enough to surround the jalapenos.

Cut the jalapeño peppers in half lengthwise. Rinse to remove the seeds and dry gently with a paper towel. Stuff the peppers with the remaining cheese mixture.

Mold the biscuit patties around the stuffed jalapenos, sealing to enclose them.

In a small bowl, beat the eggs with the water. Place the Shake 'n Bake on a dinner plate.

Roll the patties in the egg mixture, then in the Shake 'n Bake. Place in the prepared baking dish. Bake for 25 minutes or until done.

Serves 12

Seasonings, Salsas, and Sauces

Adobado

This is a traditional Mexican barbeque sauce.

6 ancho chiles, wiped clean
¼ cup white vinegar
1 cup water
2 tbsp. olive oil
1 medium onion, thinly sliced
3 garlic cloves, sliced
½ tbsp. ground cumin
2 cups chicken broth
1 tbsp. brown sugar
2 tbsp. freshly squeezed orange juice
2 tbsp. freshly squeezed lemon juice
1 tbsp. tomato paste
½ tbsp. salt
⅛ tsp. black pepper

Briefly toast the chiles directly over a medium gas flame or in a skillet until soft and brown, turning frequently to avoid scorching.

Transfer the toasted chiles to a saucepan. Add the vinegar and water. Bring to a boil, then reduce the heat to low and simmer for 10 minutes to soften the chiles.

Transfer the mixture to a blender. Purée until it is a smooth paste that is the consistency of barbeque sauce. Add 1 or 2 tbsp. of water if necessary to thin. Set aside.

Heat the olive oil in a medium saucepan over medium-high heat. Sauté the onion until it is golden brown, about 10 minutes.

Stir in the garlic and sauté for 1 to 2 minutes.

Stir in the cumin and sauté for another minute.

Add the chicken broth and reserved paste. Bring to a boil, then reduce heat to low and simmer for 20 minutes.

While this is cooking, mix together the brown sugar, orange juice, lemon juice, tomato paste, salt, and pepper in a small bowl to form a paste. Add to the broth mixture and simmer for 15 more minutes.

Adobo

This versatile chile-vinegar paste is used for marinating pork chops or steaks before broiling or grilling. It can be added to chili and used as a seasoning in many other recipes.

1 small head garlic
5 ancho chiles
2 pasilla chiles
1 tbsp. dried oregano
1 tsp. cumin seeds
6 cloves
1 tsp. coriander seeds
1 4" cinnamon stick
2 tsp. salt
½ cup white wine vinegar

Preheat the oven to 350 degrees.

Cut a thin slice off the top of the head of garlic so that the inside of each clove is exposed. Wrap the head of garlic in aluminum foil. Place in the oven and roast for 45 minutes to 1 hour or until the garlic is soft.

While the garlic is roasting, slit the chiles and scrape out the seeds. Put the chiles in a blender. Add the oregano, cumin seeds, cloves, coriander seeds, cinnamon stick, and salt. Blend into a fine powder.

When the garlic is cool enough to handle, squeeze the garlic pulp out of each clove and grind it into the spice mix.

Add the vinegar to the garlic mixture and blend until it becomes a smooth paste.

Spoon the mixture into a bowl and let stand for 1 hour to allow the flavors to blend. Refrigerate any unused portion.

Chili Powder

Instead of shaking out your chili powder from a store-bought spice bottle, make your own. San Antonio is famous for chili, and this homemade blend will spice up more dishes than chili. If you're keen on winning a chili cook-off, this could be your secret ingredient.

3 tbsp. ancho chile powder
1 tbsp. ground cumin
2 tsp. dried oregano
1 tsp. ground coriander
1 tsp. black pepper
1 tsp. salt

Mix all of the ingredients together. Store in a sealed jar.

Southwest Seasonings

Use as a dry rub for chicken, beef, or pork before you grill or to season cooked chicken and beef when you shred them for tacos. Shake this into baked potatoes, rice, or vegetables. Stir it into soups and chili. Mix it with sour cream to make a dip.

1 tsp. garlic powder
1 tsp. ground cumin
½ tsp. dried oregano
½ tsp. finely chopped cilantro
⅛ tsp. cayenne pepper

Mix all ingredients together in a small bowl. Store in a sealed jar.

Taco Seasoning

Instead of using the packaged mix, make your own taco seasoning.

2 tbsp. chili powder
1½ tbsp. cumin
1½ tbsp. paprika
1 tbsp. onion powder
1 tbsp. garlic powder
¼ tsp. cayenne pepper

Combine all the ingredients in an airtight container. Cover with a tight-fitting lid and store in the pantry. Use 2 tbsp. to flavor 1 lb. of ground beef.

Black Bean Salsa

Salsa comes in all shapes and forms.

1 avocado, peeled, pitted, and diced
3 to 4 tbsp. lime juice
1 large tomato, chopped
½ red bell pepper, diced
2 jalapeño peppers, seeded and diced
½ red onion, finely chopped
2 to 3 tbsp. olive oil
½ tsp. ground cumin
¼ cup cilantro, chopped
1 15 oz. can black beans, drained and rinsed
½ cup cooked corn
Salt and black pepper to taste
Tortilla chips

In a medium-size bowl, toss the diced avocado with the lime juice.

Add all the remaining ingredients except for the tortilla chips. Cover and chill for at least 2 hours.

Serve with tortilla chips.

Serves 4

Chipotle Salsa

3 cups chopped tomatoes
¾ cup freshly chopped cilantro
3 tbsp. fresh lime juice
1½ tbsp. chopped canned chipotle chiles in adobo sauce*
1½ tsp. ground cumin
Salt and black pepper to taste

Combine all the ingredients in a medium bowl.

Serves 4

*Canned chipotle chiles in adobo sauce are available in the ethnic aisle in grocery stores.

Simply Salsa

Serve this salsa with tortilla chips. It's also great on tacos. My daughter, Jaime, loves salsa on just about everything so she makes a big batch and stores it in small plastic bowls in the freezer. When she wants salsa, she heats it up in the microwave.

2 medium tomatoes
1 medium white onion, cut in half
8 to 10 garlic cloves
3 tomatillos, husked
3 jalapeño peppers, stemmed, seeded, and cut in half
4 serrano peppers, stemmed, seeded, and cut in half

Place the tomatoes, onion, garlic, tomatillos, jalapeños, and serrano peppers in a large saucepan. Cover with water. Bring to a boil and let boil for 10 minutes.

Place the ingredients in a blender and blend to desired consistency. If desired, season to taste with salt.

Serves 6

Chipotle Sauce

There are so many ways to use this sauce. It's terrific on top of chicken or beef. A spoonful or two stirred into a bowl of chili adds both heat and zip. This is also a great sauce to use for Huevos Rancheros.

1 medium onion, coarsely chopped
7 dried chipotle chiles, stemmed, or use 3 canned chipotle chiles
8 roma tomatoes, cored and coarsely chopped
10 garlic cloves, peeled
3 cups water
2 tsp. salt
½ tsp. black pepper
1 tsp. sugar

Combine all the ingredients in a medium saucepan. Bring to a boil, then reduce the heat and simmer, uncovered, for 20 minutes, stirring occasionally.

Pour the mixture into a blender and purée until smooth. Strain.

Serves 6

Jalapeño Sauce

This sauce is great on top of chicken or fish.

1 tbsp. butter
½ cup chopped onion
½ cup chopped green bell pepper
1 jalapeño pepper, chopped
1 large garlic clove, chopped
1½ tsp. ground cumin
¼ tsp. cayenne pepper
2 cups chicken broth
1 8 oz. can tomato sauce
¼ cup freshly chopped cilantro

Melt the butter in a 12" skillet over medium heat. Add the onion, green bell pepper, jalapeño, garlic, cumin, and cayenne pepper. Sauté until the vegetables are softened, about 7 minutes.

Add the broth and tomato sauce. Cook for 20 minutes or until the sauce thickens, stirring frequently.

Mix in the cilantro.

Serves 6

Ranchero Sauce

You may want to double or triple this recipe. Ranchero Sauce goes great with so many dishes and is the base for several recipes in this cookbook.

1 tbsp. olive oil
1 cup finely chopped onion
1 tsp. finely chopped garlic
4 medium tomatoes, peeled and diced
1 jalapeño pepper, seeded and finely diced
¼ cup chicken broth
1 tsp. chopped cilantro
¼ tsp. chili powder

Heat the oil in a 12" skillet over medium heat. Add the onion and garlic. Sauté until soft.

Add the tomatoes and jalapeño. Stir in the chicken broth. Add the cilantro and chili powder. Simmer for 10 to 15 minutes, stirring occasionally.

Serves 4

Roasted Poblano Sauce

This sauce tastes great over grilled chicken, fish, steak, or rice.

3 jalapeño peppers
10 poblano peppers
1 tbsp. vegetable oil
½ cup chopped garlic
1 medium onion, coarsely chopped
3 tomatoes, cored and coarsely chopped
1½ cups cilantro leaves
3 tbsp. chicken bouillon
2 cups half-and-half
2 cups heavy cream

Roast the jalapeño and poblano peppers over an open flame. Set aside. When cool, remove and discard charred skins, seeds, and stems. Chop the peppers coarsely.

Heat the oil in a 12" skillet over medium heat, then add the garlic, onion, tomatoes, and cilantro leaves. Sauté until the vegetables are softened, about 5 minutes.

Add the reserved peppers to the sautéed vegetables.

Reduce the heat to low and add the chicken bouillon, half-and-half, and heavy cream. Stir well to combine. Simmer until heated through. Pour the contents into a blender and process until smooth. This may be done in batches.

Serves 6

San Antonio Sauce

Instead of using canned tomato sauce, make your own to add zip to any recipe that calls for tomato sauce. It's great over Huevos Rancheros, meatloaf, or stuffed poblano peppers. You can also substitute this sauce in any recipe that calls for Ranchero Sauce.

4 large tomatoes
2 tbsp. butter
2 tbsp. olive oil
1 large onion, chopped
2 garlic cloves, chopped
2 jalapeño peppers, seeded and chopped
1 serrano pepper, seeded and chopped
⅓ cup lime juice
½ cup chicken broth
½ tsp. salt
¼ tsp. black pepper
¼ tsp. Tabasco® sauce
¼ tsp. cumin
¼ tsp. chili powder
1 tbsp. chopped cilantro

Preheat the broiler. Place the tomatoes in a shallow baking pan about 5 inches from the heat. Broil for 5 minutes, then turn over and broil on the other side for 3 minutes. Remove and let cool, then core, peel, coarsely chop, and place in a food processor, along with the juices.

Melt the butter with the oil in a 12" skillet over medium heat. Add the onion, garlic, jalapeños, and serrano peppers. Sauté until soft. Transfer to the food processor. Purée with the tomato mixture.

Return the puréed mixture to the skillet. Add the lime juice, chicken broth, salt, black pepper, Tabasco® sauce, cumin, chili powder, and cilantro. Bring to a boil, then reduce the heat and simmer, uncovered, for 30 minutes.

Serves 4

Serrano Sauce

Roasting gives this sauce a nice, complex flavor. If you're in a hurry, just leave it chunky and serve it fresh. This sauce is great served with tortilla chips or drizzled over fish or chicken.

1 lb. roma tomatoes, cored
6 garlic cloves, peeled
2 serrano peppers, stemmed and seeded
1 medium onion, cut into ½" slices
2 tbsp. olive oil
1 cup tomato juice
1 tsp. salt
Black pepper to taste

Preheat the broiler.

Place the tomatoes, garlic, serrano peppers, and onion on a foil-lined baking sheet. Drizzle with olive oil. Broil 6 to 8 inches from the heat for about 12 minutes, turning frequently with tongs, until evenly charred.

Transfer the vegetables and any accumulated juices to a blender.

Add the tomato juice, salt, and pepper. Purée, in batches if necessary, until smooth.

Pour into a medium saucepan. Bring to a boil, then reduce the heat and simmer, uncovered, for 5 minutes. Season with additional salt and pepper if desired.

Serves 4

Texas BBQ Sauce

The year-round warm weather in San Antonio is great for outdoor grilling. Brush this sauce over ribs, chicken, pork, or beef.

- 1¼ cups ketchup
- ½ cup brown sugar, lightly packed
- 1 tbsp. prepared mustard
- ½ cup Worcestershire sauce
- ½ cup lemon juice
- ¼ cup water
- 1 garlic clove, minced
- ¼ cup butter
- 1 jalapeño pepper, stemmed, seeded, and diced

Combine all the ingredients in a medium saucepan. Simmer for 15 to 20 minutes to blend the flavors.

Serves 4

Tomatillo Sauce

You can use this for chicken verde, add it to tacos, or serve as a salsa with tortilla chips.

- 1 lb. fresh tomatillos, husked and coarsely chopped
- ¼ cup water
- ⅓ cup loosely packed cilantro
- 2 garlic cloves, chopped
- ½ cup chopped green onion
- 1 serrano pepper, roasted, peeled, seeded, and diced
- 1 jalapeño pepper, seeded and finely diced
- 1 tsp. sugar
- 1 8 oz. container sour cream

Place the tomatillos and water in a medium-size saucepan. Cook over medium heat for 15 to 20 minutes. Let cool.

Place the tomatillo mixture in a food processor. Add the cilantro, garlic, green onion, serrano and jalapeño peppers, sugar, and sour cream. Purée until smooth.

Serves 4

Sweets and Treats

Apple Enchiladas

If you like apple pie, you'll love these apple enchiladas.

1 20 oz. can sliced pie apples (not pie filling), drained and liquid reserved
Water, as needed
10 fresh flour tortillas at room temperature
2 tbsp. ground cinnamon
⅓ cup butter
½ cup sugar
½ cup light brown sugar, packed

Lightly spray a 13x9" baking dish with butter-flavored cooking spray. Set aside.

Add enough water to the reserved apple liquid to measure ½ cup. Set aside.

Spoon the fruit down the center of each tortilla. Sprinkle with cinnamon. Roll and place seam side down in the prepared baking dish.

In a medium-size saucepan, bring the butter, both sugars, and apple liquid to a boil. Reduce the heat and simmer for 3 minutes, stirring constantly. Pour the butter mixture over the enchiladas and let stand for 30 minutes.

Preheat the oven to 350 degrees. Bake, uncovered, for 20 minutes.

Serves 10

Buñuelos

Buñuelos are Mexican fritters that can be sweet or savory.

1½ cups all-purpose flour
1 tsp. baking powder
¼ tsp. salt
1 tbsp. brown sugar
1 medium egg, beaten
2 tbsp. butter, melted
½ cup evaporated milk
Vegetable oil, for frying

Sift the flour, baking powder, and salt together in a large bowl. Stir in the brown sugar.

Beat in the egg, butter, and evaporated milk to form a soft, smooth dough.

Shape the dough into 8 balls, then flatten them to make cakes.

Heat the oil in a deep frying pan. Fry the cakes, in batches, for 4 to 5 minutes, turning once, or until they are golden brown and puffed. Remove with a slotted spoon and drain on paper towels.

Serves 12

Churros

Churros are often referred to as Spanish doughnuts.

1 cup water
3 tbsp. butter, diced
2 tbsp. brown sugar
Pinch of salt
1⅛ cups all-purpose flour
1 tsp. ground cinnamon, plus more for dusting
1 tsp. vanilla extract
2 medium eggs
Vegetable oil, for frying
Confectioners' or superfine sugar, for dusting

Heat the water, butter, brown sugar, and salt in a saucepan over medium heat until the butter has melted.

Add the flour all at once, cinnamon, and vanilla extract. Remove the pan from the heat and beat rapidly until the mixture pulls away from the side of the pan.

Let cool slightly, then beat in the eggs, one at a time, beating well after each addition, until the mixture is thick and smooth. Spoon the mixture into a pastry bag fitted with a wide star tip.

Heat the oil in a deep frying pan. Pipe 5" lengths of the dough into the oil. Deep fry for 2 minutes on each side or until golden brown. Remove with a slotted spoon and drain on paper towels.

Dust the churros with confectioners' sugar and a light topping of cinnamon.

Serves 12

Fabulous Flan

There are many recipes for flan. This one is easy and tastes great.

- 1 14 oz. can sweetened condensed milk
- 1 12 oz. can evaporated milk
- 1 4 oz. container cream cheese
- 7 medium eggs
- 1 tsp. vanilla extract
- 2 cups sugar

Preheat the oven to 350 degrees.

For the custard, combine milks, cream cheese, eggs, and vanilla extract in a blender. Process until smooth.

For the caramel, place the sugar in a saucepan. Cook over low heat, stirring gently until the sugar has melted and turned golden brown. Immediately pour into a 9" round pie plate.

Pour the custard mixture over the caramel.

Put the pie plate into a larger baking pan. Add ½" of boiling water to the larger pan. This is called a water bath. Bake for 2 hours or until firm.

Remove from the oven and let cool. Once cool, run a knife around the edges of the flan and invert onto a serving platter. Refrigerate until chilled.

Serves 6

Cuban Flan Heroico

Sally Buchanan, vice president of the Kangaroo Court Restaurants of Texas, Inc., offers this recipe for flan served at the Original Mexican Restaurant & Bar (www.originalmexican.com). They are also famous for their fajitas.

½ cup sugar
1 16 oz. block cream cheese
1 14 oz. can condensed milk
28 oz. whole milk
4 large eggs
2 tsp. vanilla extract

Preheat the oven to 350 degrees.

To caramelize the sugar, heat the sugar over low heat in a stainless-steel saucepan, stirring constantly with a long-handled wooden spoon until it turns a golden brown. This process may take up to 10 minutes. Watch carefully because the sugar can turn from golden to burned very quickly. Pour the caramel into a 2-qt. round Pyrex dish or a 9" glass pie pan and twirl it around to cover the bottom and sides of the dish. Set aside.

Using a hand mixer, beat the cream cheese until smooth. Blend the condensed milk into the cream cheese.

In a separate bowl, using the condensed milk can as a measure, pour two cans worth of whole milk. Beat the eggs and vanilla extract into the milk. Pour this mixture into the cream cheese-condensed milk mixture and continue blending until mixture is incorporated.

Pour this mixture into the Pyrex dish with the caramelized sugar. Place the Pyrex dish in a large pan on the middle rack of the oven. Pour enough boiling water into the pan to come halfway up the sides of the bowl. Bake the flan for about 1 hour or until a knife inserted in the center comes out clean.

Remove from the oven and place in the microwave. Cook on medium for 8 minutes, making a quarter turn every two minutes if the machine does not have a carousel. When done, loosen the custard from the sides of the Pyrex dish and rotate the dish to cover the underside of the flan with melted caramel. Refrigerate for 4 to 6 hours.

To serve, cover chilled flan with a dinner-size plate and invert. Slice into 8 wedges. This particular flan is solid, keeps its shape on a plate, and has the consistency of a cheesecake without a crust.

Serves 6

Chocolate-Kahlúa Flan

Kahlúa is a Mexican coffee-flavored liqueur.

- 1 14 oz. can sweetened condensed milk
- 1 12 oz. can evaporated milk
- 3 oz. semisweet chocolate, chopped
- 2 tbsp. cream cheese, at room temperature
- 2 tbsp. Kahlúa
- ½ tsp. ground cinnamon
- ⅛ tsp. salt
- 3 large eggs, beaten

Preheat the oven to 350 degrees. Arrange 6 ¾-cup custard cups in a 13x9" baking dish. Set aside.

Pour the condensed milk and the evaporated milk into a medium saucepan. Bring to a simmer over low heat, stirring often.

Remove the pan from the heat. Add the chocolate, cream cheese, Kahlúa, cinnamon, and salt. Whisk until the chocolate is melted and the mixture is smooth.

Whisk in the eggs, one at a time.

Divide the mixture among the custard cups. Pour enough hot water into the baking dish to come halfway up the sides of the cups. Bake for 35 minutes or until set in the center. Remove the cups and chill in the refrigerator, uncovered, until very cold and firm, at least 3 hours.

Serves 6

Kahlúa Cheesecake

Graham Cracker Crust:

1¼ cups finely crushed graham cracker crumbs
½ cup finely chopped walnuts
2 tbsp. brown sugar
1 tsp. ground cinnamon
3 tbsp. canola oil

Kahlúa Filling:

1 16 oz. container cream cheese
1 cup ricotta cheese
½ cup sugar
2 large egg whites
½ cup sour cream
3 tbsp. Kahlúa
2 tsp. pure vanilla extract

Preheat the oven to 350 degrees.

For Graham Cracker Crust: In a large mixing bowl, combine the graham cracker crumbs, walnuts, brown sugar, cinnamon, and canola oil. Mix until well blended. Transfer to a 9" pie pan and press crumbs evenly over the bottom and up the sides. Bake the pie shell for 9 minutes or until it is slightly firm to the touch. Remove from the oven and let cool before filling.

For Kahlúa Filling: Place the cream cheese and ricotta cheese in a large bowl. Beat with an electric mixer on medium speed until the mixture is creamy.

Add the sugar and beat for 30 more seconds.

Add the egg whites, sour cream, Kahlúa, and vanilla extract. Beat until well blended.

Pour the filling into the crust and bake for 40 minutes or until the center of the cheesecake is almost firm. (It will firm up as it cools.) Let cool to room temperature, then refrigerate for at least 4 hours before serving. Refrigerate leftovers.

Serves 6

Kahlúa Cookies

2½ cups all-purpose flour
2 tsp. baking powder
½ tsp. salt
1½ cups sugar
½ cup brown sugar
¾ cup cocoa
½ cup butter, melted
¼ cup vegetable oil
¼ cup Kahlúa
1 tsp. vanilla extract
4 large eggs
Confectioners' sugar

In a large mixing bowl, combine the flour, baking powder, salt, sugar, brown sugar, and cocoa.

In a separate medium-size bowl, whisk together the melted butter, oil, Kahlúa, vanilla extract, and eggs.

Pour the liquid mixture into the dry ingredients. Mix well. Chill the dough 12 hours or overnight.

When ready to bake, preheat the oven to 350 degrees. Lightly butter a cookie sheet. Sprinkle the confectioners' sugar on a dinner plate.

Using a melon baller or a small scooper, make 1 cookie at a time, rolling it in the confectioners' sugar to coat.

Place the cookies on the prepared baking sheet 1½" apart. Bake for 10 to 12 minutes or just until the cookie is set and the centers are not liquid. Do not overbake. When the cookies are cooled, they will puff up and crack. Cool 5 minutes on a baking sheet, then remove to a plate. Do not stack cookies for at least 1 hour.

Yields 3 dozen

Mocha Coffee Cookies

2 oz. unsweetened chocolate, coarsely chopped
4 oz. bittersweet chocolate, coarsely chopped
3 tbsp. butter
¼ cup plus 1 tbsp. flour
¼ tsp. baking powder
¼ tsp. salt
2 large eggs
¾ cup sugar
1 tsp. vanilla extract
2 tbsp. Kahlúa
2 tbsp. finely ground espresso beans
⅔ cup semisweet chocolate chips
¾ cup powdered sugar

Preheat the oven to 350 degrees. Line two cookie sheets with parchment paper. Set aside.

Combine both chocolates with butter in a small saucepan. Cook over low heat, stirring occasionally, until melted and smooth. Set aside to cool.

In a medium-size bowl, sift together the flour, baking powder, and salt.

In a large bowl, slowly beat the eggs and sugar with an electric mixer until pale and thick, about 5 minutes.

Beat in the vanilla extract, Kahlúa, and espresso beans. Pour in the melted chocolate. Fold to combine. Add the flour mixture. Fold until the flour disappears. Stir in the chocolate chips. The dough will be very loose.

Drop about 1 tbsp. of the batter for each cookie, spaced 1½" apart, on the lined cookie sheets.

Sprinkle each cookie generously with powdered sugar through a sieve until the cookies are evenly coated and thoroughly white.

Bake for 8 to 10 minutes or until the tops are cracked and the cookies are slightly puffed.

Let cool on the cookie sheet for 10 minutes, then transfer the cookies to racks to completely cool.

Yields 2 dozen

Mexican Brownies

1 19.8 oz. package brownie mix, plus ingredients to prepare brownies
2 tsp. ground cinnamon
1 8 oz. package cream cheese, softened
2 tbsp. confectioners' sugar
½ cup dulce de leche*

Prepare and bake the brownies according to the package directions, adding cinnamon to the batter. Cool completely.

Place the cream cheese in a medium-size bowl. Beat with an electric mixer on medium speed until smooth.

Add the confectioners' sugar and dulce de leche. Beat until well mixed and creamy.

Frost the brownies with the dulce de leche icing.

Serves 8

*Dulce de leche is a caramelized condensed milk. It is sold in cans. You can make your own by heating 1 cup whole milk and ½ cup sugar just to a boil, then reduce the heat to medium low and cook for 30 minutes or until the mixture is caramel in color, stirring occasionally. Remove the pan from the heat and let cool completely. Stir in ¼ tsp. vanilla extract. If you are using homemade dulce de leche, omit the confectioners' sugar in this recipe.

Brown Sugar Brownies

Brownies:
4 oz. unsweetened chocolate, chopped
½ cup unsalted butter
1¼ cups golden brown sugar, packed
1 tbsp. ground cinnamon
¼ tsp. salt
3 large eggs
1 tsp. vanilla extract
¾ cup all-purpose flour
1 cup milk chocolate chips

Brown Sugar Topping:
1 cup golden brown sugar, packed
¼ cup whipping cream
1 tbsp. unsalted butter
¾ tbsp. vanilla extract
½ cup sliced almonds

Preheat the oven to 325 degrees. Line an 8" square baking dish with aluminum foil, with the foil extending over the sides. Set aside.

For Brownies: Place the chocolate and butter in a large saucepan over low heat. Stir until the mixture is melted and smooth. Remove the pan from the heat and let cool for 5 minutes.

Whisk in the sugar, cinnamon, and salt.

Whisk in the eggs, one at a time.

Whisk in the vanilla extract. Continue to whisk until the batter is smooth, about 2 minutes.

Add the flour and mix just until blended.

Stir in the chocolate chips. Pour the batter into the prepared baking dish. Smooth the surface. Bake for 35 minutes or until a knife inserted in the center comes out with a few moist crumbs attached.

For Brown Sugar Topping: Whisk the sugar, cream, and butter in a small saucepan over medium heat until the mixture is smooth and comes to a boil.

Remove the pan from the heat. Mix in the vanilla extract. Let cool for 10 minutes, then whisk until it is thick enough to spread. Spread over the brownies and sprinkle with almonds. Let stand until the topping sets, about 1 hour.

Using the aluminum foil as an aid, lift the brownies from the pan. Cut into 16 squares.

Serves 8

Frozen Margarita Pie

Crust:
3 cups thin salted pretzel sticks
3 tbsp. sugar
1 large egg white
1 tbsp. canola oil
1 tbsp. water

Filling:
1 14 oz. can sweetened condensed milk
½ cup lime juice
2 tbsp. tequila
1 tsp. freshly grated lime zest
2 drops green food coloring
6 tbsp. warm water
2 tbsp. powdered egg whites*
Pinch cream of tartar
¼ cup sugar
½ cup whipping cream

Sour Cream Topping:
⅓ cup sour cream
1½ tbsp. sugar
Lime slices

Preheat the oven to 350 degrees. Lightly spray a 9" glass pie pan with nonstick cooking spray. Set aside.

For Crust: Combine the pretzels and sugar in a food processor and process until finely ground.

Add the egg white, oil, and water. Pulse until moistened. Press the mixture firmly into the bottom and sides of the prepared pan. Bake for 10 minutes. Cool completely on a wire rack.

For Filling: Whisk the condensed milk, lime juice, tequila, lime zest, and food coloring in a medium bowl until smooth. Set aside.

Combine the warm water, powdered egg whites, and cream of tartar in a separate mixing bowl. Stir gently until the egg whites are dissolved, about 2 minutes. Beat with an electric mixer on medium-high speed until soft peaks form. Gradually add the sugar, beating until stiff and glossy.

Beat the cream in a small chilled bowl with chilled beaters on medium speed until soft peaks form.

With a rubber spatula, gently fold in the reserved condensed milk mixture into the beaten whites, then fold in the whipped cream. Pour the filling into the cooled crust. Freeze, uncovered, until firm, about 1 hour. Cover and freeze for at least 6 more hours.

Let the pie thaw in the refrigerator for 30 minutes before slicing and serving.

For Sour Cream Topping: Whisk the sour cream and sugar in a small bowl until the sugar is dissolved.

Garnish the pie with the Sour Cream Topping and lime slices.

Serves 6

*Powdered egg whites are sold in the baking or natural foods section of grocery stores.

Pecan Pie

Pecan pie is a favorite in San Antonio. Pecan trees grow all over the state of Texas. In Texas, pecan is pronounced "pa-kahn."

2 large eggs
⅔ cup light corn syrup
1 cup sugar
1 tbsp. melted butter
1 tbsp. all-purpose flour
½ tsp. vanilla extract
1 9" frozen pie shell, thawed
1 cup pecan halves
Cool Whip® (optional)

Preheat the oven to 350 degrees.

In a medium-size mixing bowl, lightly beat the eggs.

Add the corn syrup, sugar, melted butter, flour, and vanilla extract. Mix well.

Place the pie shell in a 9" pie pan.

Arrange the pecan halves in the bottom of the pie shell.

Pour the egg mixture over the pecans. Let stand until the pecans rise to the surface, about 2 minutes.

Place the pie in the oven and bake for 45 minutes. The pecans will glaze during baking.

Remove the pie from the oven and let it cool completely on a wire rack before cutting into 8 pie-shaped wedges. Add a dollop of whipped cream, if desired.

Serves 8

Strawberry Blossoms

Near San Antonio is Poteet, which hosts the annual Poteet Strawberry Festival (www.strawberryfestival.com). This small town is the "Strawberry Capital of Texas" and is home to the world's largest strawberry sculpture.

1 16 oz. container large strawberries
1 3 oz. package cream cheese, softened
2 tsbp. powdered sugar
1 tbsp. sour cream
Fresh mint leaves

Remove the stems from the strawberries. Cut the tops to form a flat base. Place the strawberries pointed side up on a plate. With a sharp knife, carefully slice the strawberries in half vertically through the center to within ¼" of the base.

Cut each half into 3 wedges, forming 6 petals. Do not slice through the base. Pull the petals apart slightly.

In a small bowl, beat the cream cheese, powdered sugar, and sour cream until it is light and fluffy. Fill the strawberries with this mixture.

Serve 2 to 3 strawberries on a dessert plate. Place fresh mint leaves in the center of each strawberry.

Serves 6

Index

Adobado, 213
Adobo, 214
Alamo City Pot Roast, 150
Alamo Eggs, 40
Apple Enchiladas, 225
Armadillo Biscuits, 212
Avocado Margarita, 32

Bacon Black-Eyed Peas, 72
Baked Chicken Tacos, 113
Baked Zucchini Boats, 71
Basic Black Beans, 88
Basic Cornbread, 207
Beef 'n' Black Bean Platter, 17
Beef Chimichangas, 15
Beef Enchiladas, 133
Beef Fajitas, 151
Beer 'n' Black Bean Chili, 121
Beer Beans, 89
Best Brisket, 149
Black-Eyed Peas, 72
Black-Eyed Pea Soup, 61
Black Bean Burgers, 98
Black Bean Caviar, 18
Black Bean Dip, 18
Black Bean Patties, 87
Black Bean Potato Soup, 59
Black Bean Salsa, 216
Black Bean Soup, 60
Black Bean Tortilla Bake, 154
Black Bean Tortilla Lasagna, 86
Blackened Chicken, 173
Breakfast Bake, 47
Breakfast Chile Relleno, 48
Breakfast Tacos, 39
Broccoli Skins, 96
Broiled Bean Sandwich, 100
Broiled Salsa Beans, 88
Brown Sugar Brownies, 234
Buñuelos, 226

Ceviche Salmon, 197
Charro Beans, 90
Cheddar Chicken Burritos, 102
Cheddar Cilantro Chicken, 174
Cheese-and-Potato-Stuffed Poblanos, 72
Cheese Enchiladas, 140
Cheese Enchiladas Rancheros, 145
Cheesy Chicken Enchiladas, 141
Cheesy Chiles Cornbread, 208
Cheesy Chorizo Bean Dip, 19
Cheesy Eggs Olé, 43
Chicken-Stuffed Poblanos, 182
Chicken and Bean Burritos, 103
Chicken and Black Bean Casserole, 187
Chicken and Corn Tortilla Casserole, 188
Chicken Black Bean Torta, 100
Chicken Cannellini Chili, 129
Chicken Cheddar Quesadillas, 105
Chicken Chilaquiles Casserole, 190
Chicken Chile Casserole, 189
Chicken Chiles 'n' Corn Soup, 63
Chicken Chile Skins, 96
Chicken Chili, 130
Chicken Chimichangas, 16
Chicken Chipotle Enchiladas, 142
Chicken Chipotle Mole, 175
Chicken Empanadas, 23
Chicken Enchiladas, 143
Chicken Enchilada Soup, 67
Chicken Enchiladas Rancheras, 144
Chicken Fajitas, 193
Chicken Fiesta, 176
Chicken Pinto Soup, 64
Chicken Quesadillas, 104
Chicken Salsa Chili, 126
Chicken Tortilla Chili, 126
Chicken Tortilla Soup, 62
Chicken Tostada, 116
Chicken Tostada Salad, 54
Chilaquiles Calabacitas, 76
Chile Corn Casserole, 78
Chile Rellenos with Sauce, 74

Chili Burgers, 97
Chili Corn Chip Casserole, 155
Chili Powder, 215
Chipotle-Bean Huevos Rancheros, 38
Chipotle Chicken, 181
Chipotle Chicken Chili, 131
Chipotle Chicken Quesadillas, 106
Chipotle Mushrooms, 77
Chipotle Salmon, 198
Chipotle Salsa, 217
Chipotle Sauce, 218
Chippy Cod, 200
Chocolate-Kahlúa Flan, 229
Chorizo Bean Dip, 20
Chorizo Bean Enchiladas, 138
Chorizo Calabacitas, 75
Chorizo Casserole, 166
Chorizo Cheese Dip, 20
Chorizo Chicken Casserole, 191
Chorizo Chicken Tacos, 114
Chorizo Chili, 127
Chorizo Crescents, 24
Chorizo Enchiladas, 138
Chorizo Quiche, 51
Chorizo Scrambled Eggs, 41
Chuckwagon Corn, 77
Churros, 226
Cilantro Shrimp, 203
Cinnamon Café Latte, 30
Cinnamon Hot Chocolate, 31
Cool Kahlúa Coffee, 30
Corn and Beef Tacos, 111
Corn Chip Casserole, 155
Corn Chip Chili, 122
Corn Tortillas, 210
Corpus Christi Crab Cakes, 201
Cowboy Beans, 90
Creamy Chicken Enchiladas, 148
Creamy Salsa Soup, 66
Crockpot Chili, 123
Crunchy Chicken Olé, 183
Cuban Flan Heroico, 228
Cumin Chicken Fajitas, 194

Doritos® Chicken, 177
Doritos® Dish, 58
Drunken Beans, 91

Easy Chicken Enchiladas, 145
Easy Enchilada Soup, 66
Easy Salsa Omelet, 42
Eggplant Casserole, 78
Eggs Olé, 42
Enchilada Stack, 136
Enchiladas Verdes, 146
Enticing Enchiladas, 135

Fabulous Flan, 227
Family Style, 112
Fiesta Beef Enchiladas, 137
Flour Tortillas, 211
Fredericksburg French Toast, 50
Frozen Margarita Pie, 235
Frozen Margaritas, 31

Green Chile Chili, 124
Green Chile Meatballs, 152
Green Chile Pork Stew, 69
Green Salsa Pork, 168
Grilled Chicken Quesadillas, 107
Grilled Chicken Strip Salad, 53
Grilled Chicken Wrap, 53
Guacamole, 25
Guacamole Cheese Chips, 25

Hacienda Halibut, 202
Horchata, 33
Huevos Rancheros, 37

Jalapeño Chicken, 178
Jalapeño Cornbread, 209
Jalapeño Sauce, 218

Kahlúa Cheesecake, 230
Kahlúa Coffee, 30
Kahlúa Cookies, 231

Limeade, 34

Meaty Nachos, 27
Mexican-Style Mini Pizza, 118
Mexican Brownies, 233
Mexican Chicken Chops, 169
Mexican Mocha, 29
Mexican Pork Chops, 169
Mocha Coffee Cookies, 232
Monterey Pepper Jack Chicken, 179

Nachos Grande, 26

Orange Roughy, 202

Paseo Del Rio Chili, 128
Peasant Potatoes, 80
Pecan Pie, 236
Peppered Pinto Beans, 92
Perfect Pintos, 93
Picante Corn Chili, 122
Pico Chicken Salad, 55
Pico de Gallo, 24
Pimiento Potatoes, 81
Pinto Chicken Chili, 132
Pinto Chorizo Chili, 128
Pinto Pork, 170
Poblano Cheese Potatoes, 82
Poblano Chicken, 180
Poblano Hash and Eggs, 43
Poblano Potatoes, 83
Poblano Rice, 95
Poncho Baked Potato, 84
Pork and Peppers, 167
Pork Burritos, 102
Pork Enchiladas with Tomatillo Sauce, 139
Pork Tenderloin with Greens and Black-Eyed Peas, 171
Pork Torta, 101
Pork Tostadas, 117

Queso Chili Dip, 21
Quickie Chicken Fajitas, 195
Quickie Pintos, 94
Quickie Quesadillas, 108

Ranchero Chicken, 184
Ranchero Sauce, 219
Red Rice, 94
Red Rice and Beans, 96
Refried Tortilla Casserole, 156
Rippin' Good Round Steak, 153
Roasted Poblano Sauce, 220

Salmon with Chipotle Sauce, 200
Salsa-Style Meatloaf, 160
Salsa Beef Stew, 158
Salsa Scrambled Eggs, 44
San Antonio Chicken, 185
San Antonio Sauce 221
San Antonio Skins, 85
Sangria, 34
Saucy Beef Enchiladas, 134
Serrano-Stuffed Chicken, 186
Serrano Omelet, 45
Serrano Sauce, 222
Serrano Shrimp, 204
Seven-Layer Dip, 21
Shredded Chicken Tacos, 114
Shredded Chicken Tomatillo Soup, 65
Shrimp with Chipotle Remoulade Sauce, 205
Simply Salsa, 217
Slow-Simmered Chunky Chili, 125
Slow Picante Soup, 67
Smoked Mesquite Turkey Soup, 68
Soft Beef Tacos, 110
Sour Cream Beef Enchiladas, 110
South of the Border Casserole, 157
South of the Border Chicken Salad, 56
South of the Border Salad, 56
Southwest Cornbread, 210
Southwestern Style, 202
Southwest Seasonings, 215
Steak and Corn Tacos, 112
Stewed Okra, 79
Strawberry Blossoms, 237
Stuffed Poblano Peppers, 159
Sunny-Side Eggs, 46

Taco Pie, 164
Taco Seasoning, 216
Tamale Meatloaf, 161
Tamale Pie, 162
Tejano Beef, 165
Tender Tex-Mex Pork, 166
Tequila Salmon, 199
Tequila Sunrise, 35
Terrific Taco Cups, 57
Terrific Tacos, 109
Tex-Mex Bean Dip, 22
Tex-Mex Taco Pizza, 119
Tex-Mex Turkey Burgers, 99
Texas BBQ Sauce, 223
Tomatillo Pork Stew, 65
Tomatillo Sauce, 223
Top Tostadas, 118
Tortilla Chili, 126
Tortilla Chip Chicken Casserole, 192
Turkey Tomorrow Tacos, 115

Watermelon Aqua, 35